"Skip Ryan is an accomplished worship le:
ship he is a true servant leader who know_
presence. In these rich and helpful meditations, he shares his heart on what
is central to his calling as a pastor."

      —OS GUINNESS, author of *The Call*

"Here's why you should read this book and share it with others: it carries
the life-giving aroma and wisdom of a man who is passionate, engaged, and
consumed with the worship of Jesus. Skip has lived and led for decades as a
faithful and joyful steward of our most eternal and glorious calling—the worship of the living God—and his book is filled with rich insight and practical
applications distilled from his doxological servanthood."

      —SCOTTY SMITH, Senior Pastor,
        Christ Community Church, Franklin, TN

"Worship Jesus in His joyful assembly with all His holy angels and His chosen people: Gabriel, Michael; Moses, Elijah; John, Mary, Peter, and Paul;
your own parents, and those who told you the story of Jesus. Thank the Lord
for them. Use Skip Ryan's book and its dialogue sections at the end."

      —EDMUND CLOWNEY (1917–2005), President Emeritus,
        Westminster Seminary, minister, author, mentor

"As those who know him would expect, Skip has written a little classic on
worship. It is richly expositional, profoundly theological, and eminently
practical. Our liturgists and members will use this for years to come."

      —SANDY WILLSON, Senior Minister,
        Second Presbyterian Church, Memphis, TN

Also by Joseph "Skip" Ryan:

That You May Believe: New Life in the Son
(Studies in the Gospel of John)
Crossway, 2003

BEHOLDING THE BEAUTY

OF THE LORD

Worship

JOSEPH "SKIP" RYAN

CROSSWAY BOOKS

A PUBLISHING MINISTRY OF
GOOD NEWS PUBLISHERS
WHEATON, ILLINOIS

To
E. P. C.
1917–2005

Library of Congress Cataloging-in-Publication Data

Ryan, Joseph F., 1947
  Worship : beholding the beauty of the Lord / Joseph "Skip" Ryan.
    p. cm.
  Includes bibliographical references and index.
  ISBN 1-58134-354-X (trade pbk : alk. paper)
  1. Worship. I. Title.
BV10.3.R93   2004
248.3—dc22   2004006177

VP		13	12	11	10	09	08	07	06	05
15	14	13	12	11	10	9	8	7	6	5	4	3	2	1

Contents

Preface

THE CHURCH DOES MORE than worship. She leads her people to love, teach, trust, work, offer mercy, even to suffer and to laugh. The church does more than worship, indeed. But the church cannot do less than worship. If the church does many fine things, including the spreading of the gospel, but does not worship, it is something other than the church.

Worship is the tip of the spear point of personal and cultural transformation. Without it, no genuine and lasting Christian growth can occur for any of us, nor can any meaningful change in our world take place. Worship makes the gospel more beautiful than any of our idols. Only transcendence can break the church out of the entropic tendency to reproduce the spirit of the age.

Worship is where the means of grace (Word, sacraments, prayer, and fellowship) all get in the same room at the same time. It is these means and the energy with which they are to be enjoyed that is at the center of the following essays. There is not much here about "style" or "technique" in worship. It's not that these are unimportant; it's rather that there is something far more important in our worship: reality. The single goal in this volume is to get us to hunger for reality in our worship, to taste and see that the Lord is good.

Apart from Scripture, most of my hunches about worship came from three congregations where I worshiped as a young person just out of college: Tenth Presbyterian in Philadelphia (high Reformed, grand and glorious, Word-driven); St. Paul's Episcopal Church in Darien, Connecticut (liturgical and lively, where every Sunday we celebrated Holy Communion, and the communion of the saints was holy); and the church that met as the worshiping expression of the L'Abri Fellowship in Huemoz, Switzerland (worship as the expression of hard-won community: praying, thinking, and working together).

Dr. Edmund Clowney put words to all my convictions about worship before I ever spoke one of them. His zeal for that heavenly worship where we join angels and the communion of God's people in every generation at the throne has been a *light* shining on every worship service I've ever led.

And it is the two churches I have served as minister that have given the *heat* to my practice of worship and worship leading. It is to them that I owe the deepest gratitude for helping to forge this central zeal of my calling: Trinity Presbyterian Church in Charlottesville, Virginia (Do you remember the sound of Jordan's voice reading the Ten Commandments in the candlelight at Communion in the University of Virginia chapel?); and Park Cities Presbyterian Church in Dallas (Isn't it wonderful to pray that the ceiling would open at 8:00, 9:30, and 11:00?). These two congregations of the Lord's people have drawn worship out of me and made Sundays the center point of my week and ministry life. Thank you for helping me never to lose the wonder.

For twenty-eight cumulative years, my colleagues and friends, Dorian Brown and Robert Rucker, have demonstrated for me passionate and professional excellence as worship leaders and music directors. Even more, they have trained my heart and increased my appetite for worship by their hunger for that reality that is this book's theme. I thank both of them for their certainty that music and liturgy are also worship, even as they thereby make much of Word and sacrament.

To Terri Speicher, Communications Director of Park Cities Presbyterian Church, and to Bill Deckard, Associate Editor at

Crossway, I again owe so much for persevering with me to make this volume come together.

And to the one who sits in the third row just off the middle aisle, until just recently with one or two teenagers next to her: thank you for never saying how hard it must be to be led in the worship of the One Beautiful Man by the one fallible man you know best.

Skip Ryan
Dallas
March 2005

CHAPTER ONE

Seeking One Thing of Beauty

The LORD is my light and my salvation;
 whom shall I fear?
The LORD is the stronghold of my life;
 of whom shall I be afraid?

When evildoers assail me
 to eat up my flesh,
my adversaries and foes,
 it is they who stumble and fall.

Though an army encamp against me,
 my heart shall not fear;
though war arise against me,
 yet I will be confident.

One thing have I asked of the LORD,
 that will I seek after:
that I may dwell in the house of the LORD
 all the days of my life,
to gaze upon the beauty of the LORD
 and to inquire in his temple.

For he will hide me in his shelter
 in the day of trouble;
he will conceal me under the cover of his tent;
 he will lift me high upon a rock.

And now my head shall be lifted up
 above my enemies all around me,
and I will offer in his tent
 sacrifices with shouts of joy;
I will sing and make melody to the LORD.

Hear, O LORD, when I cry aloud;
 be gracious to me and answer me!
You have said, "Seek my face."
My heart says to you,
 "Your face, LORD, do I seek."
 Hide not your face from me.
Turn not your servant away in anger,
 O you who have been my help.
Cast me not off; forsake me not,
 O God of my salvation!
For my father and my mother have forsaken me,
 but the LORD will take me in.

Teach me your way, O LORD,
 and lead me on a level path
 because of my enemies.
Give me not up to the will of my adversaries;
 for false witnesses have risen against me,
 and they breathe out violence.

I believe that I shall look upon the goodness of the LORD
 in the land of the living!
Wait for the LORD;
 be strong, and let your heart take courage;
 wait for the LORD! (Psalm 27).

IN THE YEAR 2000, Pablo Picasso's famous painting *Woman in Blue* sold for $28.6 million at Christie's Auction House in New York. Such extravagance reminds us at the very least that people desire beauty. Some people are apparently willing to pay for it.

I used to fly out of the Charlottesville, Virginia, airport quite often in the fall. As Albemarle County fell away below me, on more than one occasion my breath was literally taken out of me as an Oriental carpet of color and beauty filled my vision.

One time when my wife, Barb, and I went scuba diving a hundred feet below the water's surface, we were awed by a staggering variety and brightness of color. Since the creation of the world, that beauty was there for only sea creatures to see, until man invented a gangly concoction of regulators, respirators, and oxygen tanks that enabled human eyes to see it as well.

Why does beauty take our breath away? Why does it pull at our eyes and heart? The answer at first seems obvious: we like beautiful things. But there is a deeper reality. A quest for beauty lies within the heart of every person. We search it out, whether we actively realize it or not, and recognizing the cause of our search is actually a key to understanding our deepest longings and our true humanity.

BEAUTY IS NOT AN END IN ITSELF

Beauty tells us that there is a longing in each of us, and that there is, in fact, such a thing as ultimate beauty. God has placed in the heart of every man and woman a desire for the beautiful in order to point to the truth that ultimate beauty exists. Men and women like the apostle Paul, Augustine, St. Theresa, John Calvin, Jonathan Edwards, and C. S. Lewis followed the Lord Himself in saying that the beauty that is all around us is not an end in itself, but it points beyond itself to the fair beauty of the Lord. It is a signpost.

When Barb and I return to Charlottesville, where we lived for many years before moving to Texas, we usually fly to Richmond and drive west on I-64. About twenty miles east of town a sign says, "Charlottesville—20 miles." I restrain my excitement about returning to the place where Barb and I met, married, and had our children until I see that sign. When I see it, I know we are almost there. But wouldn't it be silly if, when we came to that sign, we pulled our rented car over, got out, and started to unpack the bags? Of course it would be. We haven't arrived at our destination, only at the sign that tells us we are on the way.

Peter Berger, a sociologist at Boston University, calls beautiful landscapes, beautiful poetry, and even beautiful people, "signals of transcendence" that point us to a greater, deeper reality than the sign itself. They point us to the Lord.

Augustine called nature "confessions of God," and he goes on to say, "For who made these lovely, mutable [changeable] things but God who is Himself unchangeable beauty."[1]

Everything that is beautiful in the world is meant to prick our hearts and tell us that there is yet greater beauty than we dare imagine. David shows in Psalm 27 that worship is what happens when we see that anything and everything that is beautiful in the world points beyond itself to the fair beauty of the Lord. Worship is what happens when we are gripped with a desire for the vision of the Lord's beauty. David proclaims, "One thing have I asked of the LORD, that will I seek after: that I may dwell in the house of the LORD all the days of my life, to gaze upon the beauty of the LORD and to inquire in his temple" (Ps. 27:4).

It is in the Lord's house where David wants to dwell, where others come to worship too. Yes, we gain glimpses of God's beauty in our private worship, but it is interesting that David implies in Psalm 27 that corporate worship fuels the flames of private worship. That concept is the reverse of what we expect. We think we need to have a good devotional time on Sunday morning so that we can really worship.

I don't know anybody who has good devotions on Sunday morning! Preachers don't have a good quiet time on Sunday morning, certainly not if they have one or more children in the house as I have had! In fact, Sunday morning seems to be the time when many families choose to fight, often on the way to church. It is tough getting everybody dressed and there at the same time. No, our corporate worship stokes the fire of our hearts so that we get up and have a good quiet time on *Monday* morning.

CONSTRAINED BY CIRCUMSTANCES

David pursues the beauty of the Lord in worship as the one thing he wants, and he does so for two reasons, according to Psalm 27: he is constrained by his circumstances, and he is controlled by his sin. The needs and struggles in David's life compel him to seek something beyond himself. Even the quickest reading of Psalm 27 tells you that David is in the midst of a lot of stress. He talks about evildoers who are devouring his flesh. He talks about a host of bad folks who want to do him serious harm. David longs for the beauty of the Lord, even as his enemies long for his life.

The best worship takes place when the heart seeks the Lord because it must: there are financial pressures that seem to have no end; the marriage just isn't working, and the energy to keep it going is diminishing; there are broken relationships with children or parents or friends, and despair that they might never be repaired; a loved one has received a diagnosis that clouds the future. We are constrained by our circumstances in this century just as David was in his. Pain causes us to know that we need the Lord more and more.

David says that he seeks the beauty of the Lord out of desperate need. He asks the Lord to hide him in His tabernacle. He has been abandoned by men to fend for himself. Even his parents have deserted him, he says. Like a man who knows he has only one true friend, he says, "The LORD will take me in" (Ps. 27:10). The pressures and adversities push David to ask for this one thing. They reduce his life to simplicity. Have you ever been there? I know you have. Simplicity is where you want just one thing.

What is confusion? It is wanting many things. Confusion is the conflict of desires. Simplicity is wanting one thing so much that you will do whatever it takes to get it. The pressures and adversities that David is experiencing push him to weigh the value of competing interests. Asking for one thing doesn't mean David can't enjoy many other things, but they must be in their order, or they must not be there at all if they rob him of the best. Charles Spurgeon says, "David has set his heart on the pearl and is ready to leave the rest."[2]

CONTROLLED BY SIN

There is a second reason why David pursues the one thing of the Lord's beauty. He also knows that he is controlled by his sin. David knows that if he is left to himself, his heart will pursue many other things. We know that about ourselves as well, that if the beauty of the Lord does not capture our hearts, it is because scuba diving or golf or the Dow Jones or our daughter's upcoming wedding captures our hearts. These things appear beautiful to us. The world is exciting, but God grows a bit dull and abstract.

John Hall, the pastor of Trinity Presbyterian Church in Charlottesville, said, "It is as if the world is in Technicolor, but Jesus is in black and white." People keep up good appearances. We say the right Christian things if we are Christians. We pat one another on the back and give our Sunday school smiles, but all the while, as John Piper puts it, "the heart beats fast for the world."[3] The allure of many things keeps pulling us away to seek beauty that ultimately cannot be beautiful for us.

Augustine said, "My sin was this, that I looked for pleasure, beauty, and truth, not in Him, but in myself and in other creatures. And that search led me instead to pain, confusion, and error."[4]

When we first moved to Dallas, we were stunned by the meticulous appearance of the yards in most neighborhoods. We couldn't believe that people put so much time, energy, and money into the landscaping around their homes. To be honest, one of the reasons is that the area around Dallas is not the most naturally beautiful part of the country. So people compensate by making their little plots as beautiful as they can.

Some of us spend a lot of our free time researching the best vacation we can ever have. I am sure that one day I am going to find the perfect place in the world, where the beach is absolutely, magnificently white, where the waves are just the right size, where the water is just the right color and temperature, where the food tastes . . .

Why do some of us do that? Why do we need green grass and pruned bushes and colorful flowers around our homes? There is within the heart of man a desire for beauty that he will pursue in any way possible, and it is because he is looking for an ultimate beauty that he cannot grasp.

What keeps us from grasping that ultimate beauty, even in worship? We must admit that we come to worship with a hundred little one-pound weights attached to our fingers and our toes, weights of preoccupation and sins that are attached to our limbs. We don't find worship rising from our hearts. We feel sodden and heavy before the Lord. We can't even stir our own hearts out of their lethargy and dullness. We must therefore search out those objects of longing in our hearts and admit that we are looking for the wrong things.

THE BEAUTY OF JESUS CHRIST REVEALED

We are so confused that we must beg for the Lord to give us the one thing we need. It is when we see that we are constrained by our circumstances and controlled by our sin that worship can actually begin to happen. It is when we see that circumstances are beyond us. It is when we start to see that sin is not a little fly to flick off our shoulder, but that the idols of our hearts have gripped us so tightly that they have become intertwined into the structure of our personalities. Sin is not something we do in this or that instance; sin is who we are. When we begin to see that we do not know how to separate ourselves from our idols, we begin to see that it takes the mighty work of God to do it. Sin is a compelling passion. Who else can separate us from that which we love in vain and replace it with what we want to love and need to love even more? Separated from vain loves, we are prepared to see that the beauty of the Lord was most revealed when that beauty was marred, when our sin marred and maimed the beauty of the Lord.

Isaiah says, "He had no form or majesty that we should look at him, and no beauty that we should desire him. He was despised and rejected by men; a man of sorrows, and acquainted with grief; and as one from whom men hide their faces he was despised, and we esteemed him not" (Isa. 53:2-3).

We don't look at Him and say, "Beautiful Savior." We look at Him and say, "Ugly." He was marred. He was maimed. You and I marred and maimed Him with all of our idolatry and sin. That is why Jesus died. Jesus died because you want to close that real estate deal more than you want anything else. Jesus died because you want to marry that person even though he is an unbeliever, and you will do anything it takes to marry him. Jesus died because you insist on holding on to that private sin, to the way you use the Internet, to what you allow your eyes to see. Either we don't want to or don't know how to give up the ugliness of the things that we put into our hearts, and it is all that ugliness that has marred and bloodied the face of Jesus Christ.

Imagine Jesus memorizing the words of Psalm 27. They are not primarily about you and me. They are about Him. Imagine Jesus saying, "evildoers assail me to eat up my flesh . . . an army encamps against me . . . false witnesses have risen against me, and they breathe out violence." Sinless though Jesus was, it is nevertheless correct to say that Jesus came under the burden of our sin. He became sin for our sake (see 2 Cor. 5:21).

When we see Jesus constrained by the circumstances of His world and controlled by our sin to go to the Cross for us, that is when worship gets awakened in us. No gospel, no worship. People do not worship God abstractly. We worship God only in the gospel, because of the gospel, in light of the gospel. It evokes and compels worship.

It is the beauty of what Christ did when He set aside His beauty and gave it up so that we might have our eyes and hearts quickened by what is truly beautiful. When we see Jesus in this way, worship is being born in our heart.

Let me apply this, first addressing pastors and worship leaders. Our task in leading worship is to present the Word and the sacraments in such a way that we really enable the congregation to see something. What is it that worshipers first see? It is not the Lord. For good or ill, they see a person standing before them. The question is, do they see that person worshiping? They have a right to expect their worship leaders to truly worship.

A worship leader must be willing to show that he is constrained by the circumstances in his life, even struggling not to permit himself to be controlled by this or that sin, and needing the gospel so much that he is going to worship the Savior who died for him. He doesn't care what people think. His goal in worship is, first, to be a worshiper himself.

When our kids were young and we tried to teach them to like broccoli, we took a little taste of it ourselves. "Mmm, good. Want some?" we would say. That is what worship leaders need to do before the congregation's eyes: "Mmm, good. Want some?" Those who lead worship must taste and see that the Lord is good and then say, "Come to the meal and join me here." This is not to suggest that worship leaders are parents and all others are children. It is simply to say that worship is an acquired taste. My goal is to make the Lord more vividly beautiful to my own heart than all *my* idolatries, so that my congregation begins to doubt the value of *their* idolatries.

Isn't that what happens? When we see someone truly worshiping the Lord, we want to find out what they are looking at. We want to know, "What is compelling her so much? Why is this thing so valuable to her that she is willing to let other things go because of it?"

Most of us who try to help ourselves and others understand the idolatry of our hearts have noticed that sin is never abstract or vague. Think about it. Sin is always concrete. We are not tempted by *sin.* We are tempted by this particular goal, that particular act. Sin is always concrete and vivid. In all of its attraction and beauty, it can be driven out, as the Puritan Thomas Chalmers tells us, only by the power of a new influence. It is expelled by something more beautiful, and there is only one thing more beautiful, that which we must seek in worship—the person of Jesus. And we must seek Him publicly as we learn to worship together. For those of us who preach the gospel and lead God's people, the challenge is to make worship so real that we taste and see the Lord in our midst.

Worship is not a matter of talking about the Lord. It is experiencing the Lord. Jonathan Edwards explains it in a wonderful way: "There is a difference between having a rational judgment that honey is sweet, and having a sense of sweetness. A man may have the former, that knows not how honey tastes; but a man cannot have the latter unless he has an idea of the taste of honey in his mind. . . . Reason may determine that a countenance is beautiful to others, it may determine that honey is sweet to others; but it will never give me a perception of its sweetness."[5] In worship, we say, "Taste the honey, do not simply discuss and analyze it." You can't analyze and worship at the same time.

I learned a lot about football when my son played in high school. I was never much of an athlete myself, so in the Lord's humor and delight, He gave me a son who is. I learned about wide receivers and the patterns that they are to run. Chris's playbook was tattered and dog-eared. He practiced. He drilled. He counted his steps before he cut left and darted to the sideline. He ran every play a dozen times Monday to Thursday. But on Friday night, when the lights were on and the stadium was electric, at his best Chris was amazingly unselfconscious as he ran fifty yards, darted to the left, looked over his shoulder, leaped horizontally through the air, grabbed the ball, and landed in the end zone—much to the cheers of his dad.

Sometimes when we worship we keep running the plays, rather than playing the game with a degree of self-forgetfulness that means we are seeking only one thing.

In the words of C. S. Lewis, "As long as you notice and have to remember the steps, you are not yet dancing but only learning to dance. A good shoe is a shoe you don't notice. Good reading becomes possible when you need not consciously think about eyes or light or print or spelling. The perfect church service would be one where we are almost unaware of it. Our attention would be on God."[6]

If we are still aware of what we are doing in worship, of what others think, of whether we like this hymn or not, of whether or not the preacher slipped by using the subjective case after a preposition, wondering why in the world Joe wore that tie with that suit, or Mary those shoes with that dress, we are not yet worshiping, longing, seeking, desiring. Worship occurs with self-forgetfulness.

Barb and I were married on a Sunday evening in 1979 in a friend's beautiful garden that overlooks the Blue Ridge Mountains. The setting, the bride—everything was beautiful except the singing of the minister. Renny could not carry a tune in a bucket. He could not put two notes together if his life depended on it. He sings in church in a loud, boisterous, noisy, and annoying way. When asked why he sings so loudly when he knows his own limitation, Renny says, "I just want to make a joyful noise before the Lord." He doesn't care what people think about his singing. He is focused beyond himself.

Worship is the seeking of one thing, what Edwards called "the soul-ravishing views of the beauty and love of Christ," our beautiful Savior. [7]

CHAPTER TWO

Worthy of Praise

Oh sing to the LORD a new song;
   sing to the LORD, all the earth!
Sing to the LORD, bless his name;
   tell of his salvation from day to day.
Declare his glory among the nations,
   his marvelous works among all the peoples!
For great is the LORD, and greatly to be praised;
   he is to be feared above all gods.
For all the gods of the peoples are worthless idols,
   but the LORD made the heavens.
Splendor and majesty are before him;
   strength and beauty are in his sanctuary.

Ascribe to the LORD, O families of the peoples,
   ascribe to the LORD glory and strength!
Ascribe to the LORD the glory due his name;
   bring an offering, and come into his courts.
Worship the LORD in the splendor of holiness;
   tremble before him, all the earth!

Say among the nations, "The LORD reigns!
   Yes, the world is established; it shall never be moved;
   he will judge the peoples with equity."

Let the heavens be glad, and let the earth rejoice;
   let the sea roar, and all that fills it;
   let the field exult, and everything in it!
Then shall all the trees of the forest sing for joy
   before the LORD, for he comes,
   for he comes to judge the earth.
He will judge the world in righteousness,
   and the peoples in his faithfulness (Psalm 96).

Oh give thanks to the LORD; call upon his name;
    make known his deeds among the peoples!
Sing to him, sing praises to him;
    tell of all his wondrous works!
Glory in his holy name;
    let the hearts of those who seek the LORD rejoice! (Ps. 105:1-3).

AS NOTED IN THE last chapter, C. S. Lewis rightly said that in worship, as in dancing, we need to stop counting the steps. Nevertheless, we do need to learn to dance. We also need to learn to worship. How do we begin to know how to worship God? Let's think about these three truths: *first,* worship is giving God His worth; *second,* worship is God giving us His presence; and, *third,* worship is seeking God until our hearts are glad.

WORSHIP IS GIVING GOD HIS WORTH

The word *worship* in the English language is from an old English word *worthship*. The idea is that as we worship, we individually see what God is worth and begin to treasure Him. We see His value.

Isn't that what happens when members of a congregation sing wonderful hymns of praise? They begin to apprehend and treasure who God is. The light of the Spirit of God is taking bits of Scripture and fusing them to their hearts in such a way that the blinders come off, and they say, "I see something of God." They are thereby motivated to lift their voices gladly in praise to Him. One way to know that our worship is genuine is to be almost caught off guard. It's as if you suddenly hear yourself saying, "I'm actually worshiping."

John Piper says, "Worship is a way of reflecting back to God the radiance of His worth."[1] We worship when our estimate of God's worth increases relative to other things. There is nothing like worship to move us forward in appreciating the value of God in an appointed and focused way. With rhythms and language that aren't always the rhythms and language of everyday work and play, we call attention to the matchless worth of God. Giving God His worth in worship is somewhat like how you value your first new car. You park away from other cars to keep the doors from getting dinged. You wash it often and forbid the children to eat in it.

Think about it. Some of the vocabulary that we use in worship, like the vocabulary of the Psalms, is not the vocabulary that we use every day. It is not street language. It is language that is rightly elevated. One danger in some modern movements of worship is that their vocabulary does not value God enough. It is as if they are trying to pull God down to a common-denominator level. I know this is a very controversial subject, but let me put it this way: in the end, the vocabulary we use in worship matches our perception of the one who is being worshiped.

That is why every worship service must center in one way or another on the gospel of Jesus Christ, God's Son—because by the gospel we see what God is worth. In the gospel, the worth of God is given to us in His Son.

What could be worth more than the righteousness of Jesus? In the hugely important theological concept of justification, Jesus takes the sin of believers, dies because of it, and gives us His righteousness, and we live because of it. In justification we receive the righteousness of Christ. What could be more valuable? What could be more precious than the righteousness of Jesus?

Many Christians believe only half the gospel—the half that says Jesus died for their sins. That is true, of course. But that is only half the gospel. The other half is that He also gave us His perfect righteousness, and we live because of it. How do we put a value on the righteousness of Jesus Christ?

This is what individual worship is, and corporate worship is really the same thing, but it is doing these things in harness with one another. When a team of horses is hitched to a wagon, not all the horses pull equally well. One or two horses can sometimes slow down the wagon. One of our goals in worship is to get more and more of us to pull together as a team.

Corporate worship is very dependent upon the worth that others are finding in Jesus, too. We can't divorce worship from fellowship. You can't say, "I can worship God. It doesn't really matter what is going on around me." It does, because the whole process will bog down if everyone isn't being lifted up by the wonder of God's worth.

WORSHIP IS GOD GIVING US HIS PRESENCE

In defining worship, it helps to understand what we are trying to do when we worship. We are seeking to bring ourselves into a palpable sense of the presence of God. God is a Person, and we come into this Person's presence. In worship we find God to be a *transcendent* Person. That means He is different. He is holy. He is distinct.

In worship we see God as higher than we are. That is why sometimes it is right for our worship vocabulary to be a bit lofty. It is not to be old-fashioned or stuffy or irrelevant, but to be appropriate. It is not always appropriate to say, "God is cool." If you are trying to teach your seven-year-old about God, it might be okay to say, "God is cool." (Though actually it would be more accurate to say, "God is hot.") But allowing our children to think along just one line without teaching them a full and biblical vocabulary of worship is a mistake. Teaching one another and teaching our children a vocabulary of worship raises the whole level of worship for us all.

Sometimes in worship services we see that God is not only transcendent, not only something very different from us, but He is also *immanent*. He is close. The whole meaning of the Incarnation is that Jesus draws close to us. He is not just high and lifted up. He is not just holy. He is all of that, but He is also close. Jesus in the gospel draws intimately close to us.

Sometimes in our worship we find that we are very good on immanence and closeness, as when somebody prays, "Jesus, we just want to thank You that You are here, and that You are really neat, and that You love us no matter what." Now that is a prayer that stresses the closeness of Jesus. It is folksy. Yet it borders somewhat on presumption. If that were the only kind of praying we did, it would indeed be presumptuous.

Sometimes worship services are good on transcendence but not so good on immanence. "Holy and Majestic Lord," "Great God of all," "Thees" and "Thous," and all of that. Some of you may pray with "Thee" and "Thou." My colleague and friend Paul Settle prays with "Thees" and "Thous," and I kid him about it every now and then. But I love to hear Paul pray because he brings me to the throne of grace.

The point is that sometimes real worship can get lost in a sea of archaic words, and worship becomes like a period piece, a performance of something that happened in 1750. Worshipers become spectators to the phenomenon, but there is no real entering into it.

Both extremes are wrong. There is a very creative tension where real worship takes place—the tension between God's transcendence and His immanence. We see it in the beautiful combination of both so fully expressed in how the Lord taught us to pray and worship: "Our Father who is in heaven." "Our Father" is close, loving, intimate. Yet He is "in heaven." He is different. The tension means that we are not in control in worship. In a certain sense we lose control.

Yet we do not want to fall off the horse on either side. Those of us who think and pray over the content of the upcoming worship service all week want to be in control in a certain way. There are things we don't want to have happen in worship.

One of the most baffling and humbling things about worship is that neither the congregation nor the pastor nor the worship leader can make worship happen. I can't make it happen in my church.

How many man-hours and woman-hours have gone into the preparation of worship all through the week at your church? Think about the choir and instrumentalists, how many people spend time preparing musically for worship. Then there are the hours of preparation that the preacher spends getting his sermon ready. There are the hours spent by those who clean the worship room and make sure that the lights are on and that the air conditioner or heat is working. A phenomenal number of hours are spent preparing for one hour or so each week in most churches.

But all of that preparation amounts to nothing if worship does not take place. "What happened?" we ask ourselves. Well, what happened is that Someone very important didn't show up. And because He didn't show up, or apparently didn't show up, we are humbled again into realizing that it is the presence of the Lord that constitutes our worship.

It is the presence of God that makes us want to worship and then defines the worship and gives expression to it. The Lord is not like us. He is different, high and holy. But He is also like us (or better, we are like Him). He is close, especially in His incarnation as Jesus. But because the Lord is both transcendent and immanent, the presence of God in worship is no simple thing. There is no formula that can just make God show up at the appointed worship times every Sunday morning.

I can actually betray my calling as a worship leader and minister by trying to manipulate my congregation into some kind of false worship that is merely emotionalism. Emotions, which are very important in worship and must be given expression, must also be balanced with truth and content so that the nature of our worship is clearly centered on the right thing, the gospel, and the right Person, the Lord. Otherwise worship is reduced to merely subjective experience.

We also know that no preacher, no worship leader, nobody can take credit for one of those times when, maybe after a communion service where the Word has been spoken, sung, and made visible in the sacrament, with contrite hearts there is honest resolve, and something real happens. Reality in worship is not something we control.

Even the artist who works on a canvas knows this. She knows that the beauty she strives for on that canvas is something beyond it. It is something she seeks to put there, but she knows that when it is captured, it is somehow bigger than she.

WORSHIP IS SEEKING GOD UNTIL OUR HEARTS ARE GLAD

Note again Psalm 105:3: "Glory in his holy name; let the hearts of those who seek the LORD rejoice!" In the 1980s and '90s there arose among American evangelical circles a lot of emphasis on quality of performance in worship. The service had to be crafted into something artistic and entertaining, with very little congregational participation—because, they said, there are people coming in from the outside who don't know the Lord, don't want to have to speak too much, and want to be entertained.

But that is not worship.

It is important, of course, that we enjoy worship—as long as our definition of *enjoy* is correct. *Enjoy* means "to take joy in." The Bible tells us to "delight yourself in the LORD . . ." (Ps. 37:4), and "be glad in the LORD, and rejoice . . ." (Ps. 32:11). In other words, we are to take into ourselves the joy of the Lord.

And the Lord Jesus who saved us is, indeed, a joyful Lord. If you were swimming at the beach and a riptide swept you out to sea, and you were saved from certain death by a grumpy lifeguard, you wouldn't care that he was grumpy. But our Savior is not a grumpy lifeguard. The message of the gospel includes not only salvation but the gladness that goes with it.

We have been given the joy of the Lord. That is repeated in the Scriptures a number of times. "These things I have spoken to you,"

Jesus says, "that my joy may be in you, and that your joy may be full" (John 15:11). The joy of the Savior in the accomplishment of your redemption is ecstatic, and the beginning place of joy for Christians in worship is not to look at our own hearts, and certainly not to try to work up some joy with hand-raising or hand-clapping. Both may be appropriate in worship, but neither, in themselves, is the way we get joy. Joy begins when we look at the joy of Jesus Christ in His obedience to the Father. "For the joy that was set before him [Jesus] endured the cross, despising the shame, and is seated at the right hand of the throne of God" (Heb. 12:2).

Jesus went to the Cross in obedience to the Father because of His hope for the joy that He would have at His reinstatement to the Father's right hand. That is the joy that is bequeathed to you. It is your inheritance in the gospel.

There are different kinds of joy. One is the kind of joy you have when your daughter marries. That is different from the kind of joy you have when you suffer for Jesus Christ in the Russian gulag, as Alexander Solzhenitsyn did. Solzhenitsyn marked his imprisonment as the beginning of joy in his life.

Jesus was joyful, but He was also the man of sorrows. The Christian gospel is the greatest thing in the whole world, if for no other reason than that it is the only place where "sorrow and joy flow mingled down." Nothing joins sorrow and gladness like the Christian gospel. So don't be too narrowly restrictive in your understanding of what joy is. It is broad and deep. If you look for it first here on earth, you will be disappointed. Look for it at the right hand of God, and then you will enjoy it, too.

Here is a way to think of it. If we aim for our satisfaction in the mere process of worship, then neither God nor we will be satisfied. But if we aim for *God's* satisfaction in worship, then we will both be satisfied. Another way to say this is that God gets the glory, and we get the joy. The Westminster Shorter Catechism's first question asks what the chief end of man is. The answer is, "To glorify God and enjoy Him forever." Some writers think that instead of the conjunction *and*, it ought to be *by*—that the chief end of man is to glorify God *by* enjoying Him forever. Do you believe that God is glorified by your joy in Him?

What if it is true that Jesus is not a grumpy lifeguard—that He is not an unhappy lifeguard who grudgingly saved you, but is full of splendid and magnificent joy in doing it? If that is true, then I think it is quite right for us to say that God is glorified by our joy in Him, particularly when we have confessed all of those other idolatries that we might substitute for God as our source of joy.

We have settled for too little. We think that joy and gladness are found in a family, a home, a second or third car, a fourth or fifth television set, a new personal computer, or the vacation trip we've been planning. We have accustomed ourselves to such meager and short-lived pleasure that our capacity for joy has become shriveled. In worship we are awakened again to true joy.

There is nothing wrong with any of the things I just listed. It is just that we should not *seek* them as the source and supply of our happiness—because that ends up making them so puny. Augustine said, "Love, and do what you will."[2] Love God and go on vacation. Love God and buy another computer. Love God and buy a third car. I don't care, as long as you are loving God. When we do that, we find that the idols are beginning to be rooted out of our hearts; and we want the Lord more than we want anything else. When we worship rightly, we seek God until our hearts are made warm and glad. We put first things first.

When we worship, we reposition the cosmos. We reorder the stars. We put everything back in its right order. What happened in the Fall? We forgot how to worship. We forgot how to put God first. In our redemption, we learn to put the right things first again, and when we worship, we celebrate the fact that God has enabled us to do that. And we do it with joy.

Worship is therefore not only reaffirming who God is but also reaffirming who we are. John Stott said, "Our greatest claim to nobility is our created capacity to know God, to be in a personal relationship with Him, to love Him and worship Him. Indeed, we are most truly human when we are on our knees before God. Sin has caused us to seek our gladness in created things rather than the Creator."[3] Sin has caused us to seek our gladness in stuff, and when we do that, we not only dishonor God, we degrade ourselves.

THE DIRECTION OF OUR AFFECTIONS

Jonathan Edwards teaches us much about worship. He said that religion consists of our affections, and that the affections are the central core that organizes our hearts, minds, and wills. But sin has caused a misdirecting of our affections toward idols.

Edwards does not define *affections* as what a person might feel toward another person or object, but as the convergence of your mind, your will, and your emotions so that they are pointed toward one good thing. Edwards said that worship consists of aligning our affections correctly until we are glad. Good worship must engage both the mind with truth and the emotion with profound feeling, he said.

First of all, we need the strong meat of truth. Sound doctrine is essential to worship. We can't worship that which we do not know. If we do not know Jesus Christ accurately, as He is given to us in the Word, we can't worship Him.

But the light of truth isn't just to inform our minds; it is also to warm our hearts and to make us want to vanquish our idols. If in worship we engage only the mind, it becomes merely intellectual exercise. I expect that you have been in a church service where you have felt that all you heard was a lecture.

On the other hand, if worship becomes sloppy and sentimental and seems directed only toward the heart, then it has no content. So

I say to preachers and to myself, "Preach to the will." The sermon should challenge the whole being of each worshiper—not just the mind, not just the emotions, but everything. Settling for one without the other turns worship into either a classroom or a catharsis, but it is not worship.

Edwards says that worship happens when our affections have been moved from idols to God, when a transformation of desires has occurred. Such transformation will be lasting because our minds are filled with strong, vigorous challenges to think. And, on the other hand, the emotions are moved so that we act on what we now know to be true. Edwards learned a lot about worship from Augustine, the great church father who lived in the fourth and fifth centuries, more than a thousand years before Edwards.

One cannot talk both meaningfully and delicately about Augustine at the same time. Here is the way he described himself: "As I grew to manhood, I was influenced with desire for a surfeit of hell's pleasures. My family made no effort to save me from my fall by marriage. Their only concern was that I should learn how to make a good speech."[4]

Augustine said that his father "took no trouble at all to see how I was growing in Your sight, O God, or whether I was chaste or not. . . ."[5]

"I went to Carthage where I found myself in the midst of a hissing caldron of lust. . . ."[6]

"I was at the top of the school of rhetoric. I was pleased with my superior status. And slowly, with conceit, it was my ambition to be a good speaker for the unhallowed and inane purpose of gratifying human vanity."[7]

But God, by His happy and sovereign grace, rid Augustine of those "fruitless joys" and replaced them with a true, sovereign joy. As Augustine expressed it, "You drove them from me and took their place. You are sweeter than all pleasure."[8]

What Augustine understood is what Freud understood in the early twentieth century: people are always motivated by joy. Freud perverted that idea, of course, but he was right on the principle. Augustine put it this way: "Every man, whatsoever his condition, desires to be happy. There is no man who does not desire this, and each one desires it with such earnestness that he prefers it to all other things."[9]

God made us to be glad. He wired us so that we would know joy. The words, hymns, confessions, and sermons in worship are all intended to show us that there is a true gladness for which we were made. Worship happens when God, by His sovereign power, does what we cannot do. He does a miracle—He pushes upon our hearts, once again, a growing recognition of all of those idols on which we have previously rested our happiness. He knocks over every idol on the altars of our hearts with the Cross, and then He polishes the altar with the blood of His Son.

By sovereign grace in worship, God plants in our hearts a new desire for Him, and He is better than anything. The gospel of His Son is more precious than anything. If God did not have the power to change our hearts from what John Calvin called "a veritable idol factory"[10] to being hearts that worship Him—if He didn't give us new eyes to see, new ears to hear, new tongues to pray—there would be no worship. The greatest thing in the world is a sovereign God who has the power to do in our hearts by the gospel of His Son what we cannot do ourselves. Praise be to God. Be glad. Be very glad, because your gladness is not dependent on you. It is dependent on Him and what He has done and is doing as He calls us to worship Him in all of His glory.

CHAPTER THREE

Soul-Ravishing Views

~⥿

Now about eight days after these sayings he took with him Peter and
John and James and went up on the mountain to pray. And as he was
praying, the appearance of his face was altered, and his clothing became
dazzling white. And behold, two men were talking with him, Moses and
Elijah, who appeared in glory and spoke of his departure, which he
was about to accomplish at Jerusalem. Now Peter and those who were
with him were heavy with sleep, but when they became fully awake they
saw his glory and the two men who stood with him. And as the men
were parting from him, Peter said to Jesus, "Master, it is good that we
are here. Let us make three tents, one for you and one for Moses and
one for Elijah"—not knowing what he said. As he was saying these
things, a cloud came and overshadowed them, and they were afraid as
they entered the cloud. And a voice came out of the cloud, saying,
"This is my Son, my Chosen One; listen to him!" And when the voice
had spoken, Jesus was found alone. And they kept silent and told no one
in those days anything of what they had seen (Luke 9:28-36).

IT HAS BEEN SAID THAT many people worship at their work, work at
their play, and play at their worship. Believers in the Lord Jesus Christ
should worship at their worship. That is the most thrilling experience
that we human beings can have, these "soul-ravishing views"[1] of the love
and beauty of God. All people are made for worship. God made the very
cells of our body, the molecules of our being. He knit us together in
such a way that we were intended for worship. By nature we are worshipers, therefore we will worship something. We were made to enjoy
what we worship. As we come to worship, our hearts should be glad.

Many years ago at my church in Virginia I passed out a brochure called "Guidelines for Worship at Trinity Church." It consisted of about fifteen couplets. Each advised the worshiper to *recognize* something and then *do* something. Just a few years ago I decided to hand it out at my church in Dallas, but I changed it significantly (see appendix 2). One of the couplets originally said that when we leave a worship service we should not ask how we *feel* but how we *did*.

I was trying to convey that the emphasis in worship should not be what we feel or experience; instead we should be asking ourselves, "How did I do? Did I worship well?"

I don't believe that anymore. It is wrong. I now believe that there is a certain sense in which it is right to ask, "Was I glad in my worship? Did worship move me?" Jonathan Edwards would have asked, "Was there heat and light?" Was I motivated by the light of the truth of the gospel in such a way that my heart and will were moved to do something? There is nothing wrong with being moved and having feelings. In fact, if you go to worship Sunday after Sunday and never feel anything but duty, then you are not worshiping.

People speak about worship as duty. "It is our highest duty," they would say. And it is. I do not deny that that is true. But when worship is only our duty, it is an empty duty. It is a duty without joy, without movement, without light.

With gratitude to John Piper, I offer this illustration:

Imagine that I arrive home on Barb's and my twenty-fifth anniversary with twenty-five roses to surprise her. I knock on the door, she opens it, and I say, "Here, these are for you."

She says, "Oh, Skip, they are beautiful! Thank you!"

I say, "Oh, no, no. That's okay. Don't mention it."

She exclaims, "Oh, but these are the most beautiful roses I've ever seen. Look, there are twenty-five of them, one for each year. Thank you, Sweetie."

I respond very matter-of-factly, "Oh, no. Please, don't mention it. It was my duty."

Dutiful roses don't work. And dutiful worship doesn't work. God wants the glad worship of willing hearts. I maintain that we do not give God glad worship until a sovereign God regenerates our hearts, makes us new people, and makes us capable of having the capacity for worship that we've never had before. But once God does it, He does not want the dutiful, grudging worship that might flow out of us. He wants our hearts.

When someone does something nice for you, and you thank them, do they ever respond that, "It was my pleasure"? It may be said casually as a nice response when somebody thanks you for something. But if it is said with true sincerity, then joy is coupled with the act itself in such a way that the joy completes or fulfills the meaning of the action. It is the fact that you take joy in the giving, in the kind deed, that makes it so meaningful. It is not just duty. To be sure, there are times when we do things just out of duty. We do them just because they are the right thing to do, because we should. Truly, life is full of duty; but worship should be full of joy as we do it, not simply because we ought to, but because we want to do it.

We are made for worship, and we are made to enjoy what we worship. A wild and happy cheer at our son's soccer game or daughter's volleyball game shows us that we love to praise and exalt what is important to us. We praise what we love! The world is full of that kind of praise—praise for our team, our wife or husband, our children or grandchildren, our political candidates, or the exceptional accomplishments of a friend. There is a joy in praise, and it should be so. The instinct of praise is very close to what worship is, and the impulse for worship is that God made us for worship.

As Augustine famously said, "Our hearts are restless, until they find their rest in Thee, O Lord."[2] Our hearts are restless looking for all kinds of objects of worship, until they find their rest in God. Our restlessness can be settled only by the Lord, and particularly by seeing something of His splendor and glory. In worship, we see God.

THE FELT PRESENCE OF GOD

Now obviously, "we see God" needs some explaining. God is invisible. He has no body parts. He is not visible to our eyes now. Therefore, what do we mean when we talk about "seeing God" as being the essence of our worship? Capturing these sightings of God's wonder, love, and beauty for just a moment is the essence of our worship. It is also the essence of what changes the texture of our personalities and our character. It reaches out to sin in our hearts and gives us a longing for things that are far better and far greater than any of our idols. As we saw in chapter 1, such sightings cause us to exclaim with the psalmist, "One thing have I asked of the LORD, that will I seek after: that I may dwell in the house of the LORD all the days of my life, to gaze upon the beauty of the LORD and to inquire in his temple" (Ps. 27:4). Without such beholding, worship will inevitably degenerate into performance or a ritual of duty.

Look at Luke 9:28-36, where we are told about the Transfiguration of Jesus Christ. Mountains are very important in the Bible. They are places where the beholding of the Lord takes place. All throughout the Bible men and women get glimpses of God and of their deepest identity as human beings on mountains. We speak of having a mountaintop experience, especially at events like a retreat or a conference.

Throughout Scripture, worship takes place on mountains. It is the place where God reveals Himself; where people get sightings of His love, His wonder, and His beauty; where His character is disclosed; where His majesty is demonstrated; and, above all else, where His glory is shown. When we say glory, we mean everything that God is—His love, His beauty, His wonder, the greatness of His person, the magnificence of His work. All of that is summarized in the word *glory*.

Moses goes to Mount Sinai to receive the Word of God. There he sees something of the glory of God. Jesus teaches the truth on a mountain. We call it the Mount of Beatitudes. Remember in Genesis 22 that God commands Abraham to sacrifice Isaac on Mount Moriah. After the Resurrection, Jesus charges all of His disciples to go into the world, to baptize, to teach, and to obey all that He told them to do; He gives those commands on a mountaintop, presumably Mount Olivet, just outside of Jerusalem. And at the end of Matthew's Gospel, it says that the disciples met Jesus on that mountain, and they worshiped Him.

All of these and many more mountaintop scenes in Scripture are characterized by two realities: First, the presence of God is perceived. It is better, however, to say something stronger than a nice, safe term like *perceived*. It is better to say that the presence of God is *felt*.

There is nothing wrong with feelings, as long as they are generated by the truth, as long as they are not made up, as long as they are not sloppy sentiments or a conflagration of one's emotional needs at that moment. The presence of God is *felt* in the Bible. The presence of God is *tasted* in the Bible. The presence of God is *touched* in the Bible.

Not only is the presence of God felt; the words of God are heard, and it is by means of the words of God that the people of God come to see Him for who He truly is. When God gives us His presence, He gives us His Word. In fact, He does not give us His presence apart from His Word. Any manifestation of the presence of God apart from His Word is highly suspicious and may be false, because God has attached Himself to His Word. God has purposed to reveal Himself in words.

On the Mount of Transfiguration all of these phenomena come together. Jesus takes Peter, James, and John to the mountain, and there His appearance is changed. His garments become radiantly white. Mark's Gospel says that they become whiter than any bleach can make them (9:3). His very being is filled with light. Imagine what Peter, James, and John saw—the being of Jesus filled with light and glory.

Psalm 104:2 (NIV) says that God wraps Himself in light as with a garment. The word *wrap* is from a root word in an Old Testament language—not even Hebrew—called Acadian. It means "to darken." The psalmist is expressing poetically the seemingly contradictory idea that God darkens Himself with light. God is so glorious, so full of pure light that even light casts a shadow upon Him.

The essence of God is His glory. The Hebrew word for *glory* is *kabod*. It is onomatopoeia, because the word *kabod* sounds like what it means in English, "heavy." God's glory is weighty. God's glory really matters, compared to anything else in the world. Everything else is lightweight compared to God's glory.

CHRIST'S ETERNAL GLORY REVEALED

The Transfiguration reveals Jesus differently than Peter, James, and John had previously known Him. They see Him in all of His glory—"glory as of the only Son from the Father," as John puts it (1:14). For a moment they see Jesus with all of His outward glory regained and in all of the splendor that He had from all of eternity with God the Father.

Theologians sometimes call the incarnation of Jesus a part of His humiliation. The humiliation of Jesus is not just at the Cross. It is the whole package of His coming in the flesh: His birth, His life, His suffering, and His death. All of it was the humiliation of Jesus, because in that humiliation, Jesus' true glory was both shown and hidden.

The irony of ironies is that the glory of God was revealed in the only begotten Son when He became flesh, and yet, when Jesus became the incarnate Son, He emptied Himself of all of the outward prerogatives of His glory and hid His true glory from us. That's one of the conundrums of the Christian faith. Christ's glory is revealed and His glory is hidden at the same time, in the same Person, in the same incarnation. But while His glory is both revealed and hidden, at the Transfiguration Jesus appears to these three disciples in a dramatically different way.

This is why it is so significant that, at the beginning of the Great Commission, following His resurrection, the Conqueror of death's power says, "All authority in heaven and on earth has been given to me" (Matt. 28:18). *Given* there literally means "restored." The power that He willingly gave up in the humiliation of His incarnation is now restored to Him in preparation for His glorification. He is ready to be glorified again—we could call it "re-glorification"—because He always had glory. He had glory from before the foundation of the universe, from all eternity past with the Father. Nothing was ever lost of that glory. It was only hidden, disguised in the Incarnation. Now the fullness of the glory is going to be restored.

When Peter, James, and John go up that mountain, what they see is the power of Jesus in His eternal Sonship. They had seen Him already in the manifestation of His earthly mannishness, but now they see just a glimpse of His eternal Sonship, the way He had always been in glory with the Father. They go to the mountaintop to see Him for who He truly is. That is what we do in worship. We go to the mountaintop in worship to see Jesus for who He truly is.

The disciples have a sense of this, a perception, a set of feelings. They were asleep; now they are awake. I'll bet they were awake! Obviously their beings are flooded with that light, with a perception of Christ's glory. But there are also words! Words have to happen on the mountaintop, not just perceiving, not just feeling. What do they hear? They hear God's voice: "This is my Son, my Chosen One." "You thought you knew who my Son was, but now do you see? *This* is my beloved Son."

As God's Son, Jesus has the right to exercise rule and dominion. He is the Agent of the Father's creative work. When God made the world, He did so through His Son. His Son is both the Owner and the General Manager of the universe. The apostle Paul says, "For by him all things were created, in heaven and on earth, visible and invisible, whether thrones or dominions or rulers or authorities—all things were created through him and for him. And he is before all things, and in him all things hold together" (Col. 1:16-17).

Peter, James, and John get more than they bargained for. They think they are going on a private little discipleship retreat. "This is good. We've been asking for this," they say. These three are the most audacious of the disciples. Do you remember how they once went to Jesus (see Mark 10:35-40) and said, "When You enter Your glory in Jerusalem [imagine what they thought that glory was going to be] You'll be center stage. But we would like to be with You, one on Your right and one on Your left. You'll be in the center, Jesus. You'll be getting all the spotlight. You'll be getting the glory, but the floodlights will sort of spill over onto—well . . . us!"

Do you remember what Jesus said to them on that occasion? "You do not know what you are asking for." Then He immediately translates the glory that they expect into suffering. "Are you able to drink the cup that I will drink?"

"Oh, yes, we are. Whatever it is, we can do it. We're with You, Jesus."

The second question was, "Are you able to be baptized with the baptism with which I am baptized?"

"Oh, sure."

How distorted is our view of glory!

COMPREHENDING HIS GLORY

We do not understand glory, and we will never understand it. We will only approximate it. We will hear sermons from preachers and lessons from teachers all our lives that will try to help us understand what glory is, and we will not understand it because preachers and teachers don't understand it. We will not understand glory until that moment when we are taken into the light of God in heaven itself. Even then, if my sense of Scripture is correct, it will not be split-second understanding, but it will take *forever* to appreciate what we are apprehending in that moment. Despite popular imagery, heaven will not be boring. And if heaven is not boring, then surely worship should not be boring. Worship is a foretaste of God's heavenly presence.

Is our vision dim? Oh, yes, is it dim. Incomplete? Very incomplete. That is why there is no room for triumphalism in our Christian life. There is no room for people presuming to other Christians that they know exactly what Jesus was thinking when He spoke. He answered Peter, James, and John on the Mount. The only way we know exactly what Jesus was thinking in that moment is if Jesus speaks and Scripture tells us.

We need to be humble before the glory of God and recognize that we get it only in shadows and glimpses and brief sightings. But one second of sighting the glory of Jesus in worship can inflame a whole week, make sense of all of the mess of life, and unravel all its pain and difficulties. Worship can be many things, but it should never be boring.

Exodus 3 relates a very similar sighting of God's glory and a presumptuous response by the one who sights this glory. It is the case of Moses and the burning bush:

> Now Moses was keeping the flock of his father-in-law, Jethro, the priest of Midian, and he led his flock to the west side of the wilderness and came to Horeb, the mountain of God. And the angel of the LORD appeared to him in a flame of fire out of the midst of a bush. He looked, and behold, the bush was burning, yet it was not consumed. And Moses said, "I will turn aside to see this great sight, why the bush is not burned." When the LORD saw that he turned aside to see, God called to him out of the bush, "Moses, Moses!" (Ex. 3:1-4).

Only five times in the Bible does God repeat a person's name. Whenever it happens, it is always an indication of tremendous intimacy—God's knowing of the person involved. "Moses, Moses, I know what you are doing."

> And he said, "Here I am." Then he said, "Do not come near; take your sandals off your feet, for the place on which you are standing is holy ground." And he said, "I am the God of your father, the God of Abraham, the God of Isaac, and the God of Jacob." And Moses hid his face, for he was afraid to look at God (Ex. 3:4-6).

What is the obvious contradiction? We should long with all our hearts to look at God, but we should be afraid to look at God. Both things are true.

Moses thinks that this bush is an interesting scientific phenomenon. "Oh," he said, "I must turn and look at this. I must study it. Maybe I'll be able to figure out how this is happening. The bush is burning, but it is not consumed. This is very interesting."

God asks, "Moses, do you understand what you are looking at?" It is like Jesus' question, "Can you drink the cup that I drink?" It is like Peter's presumption on the Mount of Transfiguration: "It is great to be here with you, Jesus and Elijah and Moses. Maybe you need little tents." Luke adds parenthetically that Peter didn't know what he was saying (9:33).

Most people do not know what to say when they are confronted with the glory of God. In fact, words may be inappropriate at such a time. Moses, the scientific inquirer, is told to take the sandals off his feet because the ground on which he is standing is holy, and then God announces to him His name: "I am the God of Abraham, the God of Isaac, and the God of Jacob. I am the God who has always been. I am the God who will always be. I am the I AM God, the God who is self-sufficient, the God who needs no one, the God who is absolutely sovereign, the God who does what He pleases, the God who calls and gives life and hope where and how He pleases" (see Ex. 3:6-15). Moses the scientific inquirer becomes very quickly Moses the worshiper. He gets down on his face, and he worships One whom he is only beginning to know.

In Luke 9 we see that Peter likewise is confused. He doesn't know what to make of the glory and holiness of God. In some ways, in offering to build tents, Peter is trying psychologically to hold onto the experience. He is trying to preserve it, to control it. Maybe it is a reach, but I think he is trying to say, "This is a very good thing happening here on this mountain. I don't want it to end. Can we figure out how to bottle this and make this happen again? I'll build some tents to structure and contain the worship of God." What does God think of man-made containers to hold His worship? Not much.

Perhaps you have heard the story of Asbury College, a small Christian college in Kentucky. At a certain time several years ago, the spiritual environment on campus had been deteriorating. The students and faculty were spiritually tired. Chapel attendance was required of students every day, but it was pretty ho-hum; the students and faculty came and left routinely.

One day, as another chapel service ended and everybody was rising to leave, a student stood up in the back of the room and said, "Excuse me, could you wait just a minute? I need to say something. I stole something from my roommate last semester. My roommate is sitting over there, and I just want to say I'm sorry and I want to make restitution." The roommate stood up and said, "I forgive you."

Then another student stood up and said, "I need to say that I cheated last week on a history exam. And I am very sorry, Professor So-and-So, and I will take whatever consequences come my way." The professor stood up and said, "I need to confess to you all that I have been jealous about my use of time. I don't share it with students. I don't love students the way I used to when I felt called into teaching as a vocation."

One after another people stood up to confess, read a Scripture, pray, or begin the singing of a hymn. No one left the chapel for hours. Gradually people would go away for a little time to get something to eat or to nap, and then they would come back to the chapel. The chapel was always full, twenty-four hours a day, for seven straight days.

At the end of seven days, it was simply over, and everyone knew it. Everyone stood up, walked out, went back to classes and back to their regular routine—though, indeed, as very different people. They called it the "Asbury Revival."

Do you know what they did a year later? The trustees, faculty, and student government of Asbury College scheduled what they called and publicized as the "Second Asbury Revival." Guess who didn't show up for the second revival?

God's glory is not contained by our tents. When God's glory is revealed in the people of God in worship, God is the One who is in control, not the worshipers. This is hard for us to learn. Our worship is often like Peter's; we come to Jesus with all our attempts to be useful. We come with all of our spiritual projects, and God says, "Be quiet. This is My Son; listen to Him." We have to stop trying to talk God into how useful we are to Him.

What Do We Need to Do?

The psalmist indicated that it would not be inappropriate in worship for those so inclined to kneel at their place during a time of corporate prayer (see Ps. 95:6). Lying prostrate is a little bit more unusual now, but it is common in Scripture, as is the lifting of hands before the Lord in prayer.

None of these physical manifestations is required. There is a difference between something that is a requirement in worship and something that is an option. *Element* is the formal term Presbyterians have historically used for "that which the Bible requires" in worship. Those elements include Scripture reading, preaching, singing, praying with confession, and taking an offering.

Yes! The offering is required. The Bible says that we should be putting something in the offering plate each Lord's Day. For those of us whose income is fixed monthly, we should write four (or five) checks at the beginning of the month or one check every Saturday night, not just one check a month or quarter or year. I know that is awkward for some whose income is less predictable, but think about the command of the Lord and how to obey it.

The elements are required, but the *circumstances* of worship, to use the term that Presbyterians employ, are not. How you stand or sit or kneel, whether the minister wears a robe or blue jeans on Sunday morning, or whether you use an organ or tambourine are not matters that are absolute.

THE TENSION OF INTIMACY/SEPARATION

Jesus was different from Peter, James, and John. There is a sense in which Peter, James, and John should not have been so familiar with Jesus. Maybe they thought of Jesus as we sometimes do, as our buddy. They had spent much time with Him, they identified with Him, but now they needed to see how different He is. From this time on in the Gospel of Luke they begin to see that very thing.

Jesus' great closeness is with His Father. After the Resurrection, He doesn't say, "I ascend to our Father." He says, "I am ascending to my Father and your Father" (John 20:17). Whatever Jesus means by "Father" is something somewhat different from what we mean by Father, and therefore He has to use cumbersome language to say it. There is awesomeness about Him, even strangeness. He leads the crowd in solitude. As the disciples walk with Jesus on the road going up to Jerusalem, Jesus tells them, "Where I am going, you cannot follow." It is in the departure of Jesus on the Cross that He is most unlike His disciples.

At the Transfiguration Jesus talks to two people, Moses and Elijah, about His departure that He is about to accomplish at

Jerusalem. He is talking to two people who happen to know a lot about departures. In 2 Kings 2, Elijah and Elisha were walking and talking when there appeared a chariot and horses of fire, which separated the two of them, and Elijah was taken up by a whirlwind into heaven. That's a pretty good departure!

But how about Moses' departure? At least two million people followed him out of Egypt with Egyptian food, Egyptian clothing, Egyptian livestock, Egyptian silver, Egyptian gold, and Egyptian blessing. When the Egyptians decided to withdraw their blessing because they thought the Israelites were getting away with too much, they chased after them. Moses took his staff and put it in the Red Sea. The water separated, the Israelites got through it, the Egyptian army followed, and the water came down and drowned them all. That's a rather dramatic departure.

But the prophetic meaning of Moses' departure was even greater. Through Moses, God delivered Israel out of the bondage of being slaves into the hope of the Promised Land. Moses' departure speaks of Christ, who frees us from the slavery of sin into the liberty of being the sons of God.

So Peter, James, and John see the glory of God's Son revealed on the mountain, and that glory of Jesus is most revealed at the Cross. That is why, in the Gospel of John, the word *glory* is almost always synonymous with the suffering, death, and crucifixion of Christ.

Where do you look for the glory? The promise of God's Word is that Light shall shine out of darkness. Paul says, "For God, who said, 'Let light shine out of darkness,' has shone in our hearts to give the light of the knowledge of the glory of God in the face of Jesus Christ" (2 Cor. 4:6). Why does he say "in the face" of Jesus? Do you see the glory of Jesus when He looks at Peter after Peter denied Him? Do you see the glory of Jesus when He looks at Martha and says, "Oh, Martha, you're worried about so many things"? Do you see the glory of Jesus on His face when He hangs from the Cross? Can you imagine His face, the eternal Son of God, who had God's glory from all eternity, in such pain and agony?

There is no glory in our worship without the gospel in our lives. And, yes, the glory of God is most revealed in the gospel of Jesus' life, death, and resurrection.

You should expect soul-ravishing views of the beauty and love of Christ at your place of worship every Sunday morning, but you should expect to find them in the face of Jesus, who died for you. You will see God in your worship when you see what even the angels cannot look at—the Son, who gave His life for you.

Chapter Four

The Implications of Our Worship

IS WORSHIP AN END IN ITSELF? If we behold the beauty of the Lord in the face of the Lord Jesus Christ and long more than anything else to inquire in the temple of the Lord, isn't that the ultimate goal? Yes, it is. It is the beginning, and it is the end. Everything else in our lives should always, in some way, point to worship.

But it is equally true to say that worship can never be the end. It must always issue in obedience that brings honor to Jesus Christ.

So what does it mean on Monday morning that we worshiped in the beauty of holiness on Sunday? In order to talk about the church as a worshiping body and all the implications of the beauty of worship, we also need to think about the deepest, richest part of our past. And I don't mean the Reformation era or a hundred years ago or when we were in college. I mean two thousand years ago.

To do so, look at Peter's speech at Pentecost, in Acts 2:36-47:

> "Let all the house of Israel therefore know for certain that God has made him both Lord and Christ, this Jesus whom you crucified."
> Now when they heard this they were cut to the heart, and said to Peter and the rest of the apostles, "Brothers, what shall we do?" And Peter said to them, "Repent and be baptized every one of you in the name of Jesus Christ for the forgiveness of your sins, and you will receive the gift of the Holy Spirit. For the promise is for you and for

your children and for all who are far off, everyone whom the Lord our God calls to himself." And with many other words he bore witness and continued to exhort them, saying, "Save yourselves from this crooked generation." So those who received his word were baptized, and there were added that day about three thousand souls.

And they devoted themselves to the apostles' teaching and fellowship, to the breaking of bread and the prayers. And awe came upon every soul, and many wonders and signs were being done through the apostles. And all who believed were together and had all things in common. And they were selling their possessions and belongings and distributing the proceeds to all, as any had need. And day by day, attending the temple together and breaking bread in their homes, they received their food with glad and generous hearts, praising God and having favor with all the people. And the Lord added to their number day by day those who were being saved.

At the beginning of the book of Acts, in Acts 1:8, Jesus gives a command. He tells the eleven apostles that they are to wait until power is given to them. But when the power of the Holy Spirit comes, they are to go to Jerusalem, to Judea, to Samaria, and to "the end of the earth" with the truth of the gospel.

Then, at the beginning of chapter 2, the power of the Holy Spirit comes, and Peter proclaims the gospel with great power (as quoted, in part, above). But what do we find? The people do not obey Jesus' command to take the gospel to the whole world. In fact, they don't go anywhere at all until Acts 8. In fact, it has been said that Acts 1:8 is fulfilled by Acts 8:1. For we read in Acts 8:1 that there is a great persecution following the stoning of the saintly Stephen, and as a result all of the Christians in Jerusalem except the apostles are scattered and begin evangelizing. In fact, the words in 8:1 mimic the words of Acts 1:8: "They were all scattered throughout the regions of Judea and Samaria."

But were the believers being disobedient in the first seven chapters of the book of Acts? We want to say no. But why? Jesus said, "Go. When the power comes, go." Well, the power came, and they stayed.

However, I don't think the first seven chapters of Acts were chapters of disobedience. They were chapters of learning. In the Lord's plan, they were going to go, but they needed to learn something very important first. What they had to learn fills the first seven chapters of the book of Acts: they had to learn how to be the church. They didn't have a denominational book of church order. They didn't know anything at all about how to be a church, and they had to learn.

How do we explain the joy of these new believers? Almost every other sentence in these seven chapters is laden with joy. They broke bread in their homes, had glad and sincere hearts, praised God, and enjoyed the favor of all the people. There was a remarkable sense that the Lord was in their midst.

How do we explain that everyone was filled with awe? When God's people worship correctly, there should be awe. There should be the sense that the Lord is in our midst and is doing something not just in our worship but in preparation for, after worship, being sent out into the world. The Lord is in our midst when we gather, and the Lord is with us when we scatter.

GATHER, THEN SCATTER

There can be no scattered people of God without the gathered people of God. There can be no good works, fruit bearing, Kingdom extension, evangelism, mercy, or missions without worship. The insistence that both worship and service be brought together is unique to the Christian church. The people who worship are also the people who serve the King; the people who worship are also those who go wash feet in the world. Worship and service cannot be separated. In fact, it is the beautiful combination of those two things that produces awe.

Note that when Acts 2:43 (NIV) says, "Everyone was filled with awe," it doesn't say just the Christians were filled with awe. The Christians were a tiny minority in Jerusalem, even though there were a large number of people converted at one time. "Everyone" included the whole city. The city of Jerusalem rejoiced in the presence of the church even as it contemplated persecuting it. The essence of Christian thinking right from the very start was awe from being in the Lord's presence, and then there was awe in the city because God's people had been in His presence.

But the city would not have known the awe if God's people had not scattered, so it was incredibly important that the scattering should take place after the gathering. Then when they came back together again, which they did frequently, they licked their wounds, ministered to one another, and prayed together. Most of all, they worshiped, in order to regain the strength that they needed to be salt and light out in the city again. There is this wonderful coming and going in the early church that should characterize the church in all times.

What was the makeup of this first church? There were eleven apostles at the beginning, then Judas was replaced by Matthias. Then Acts 1 says that there were 120 of them gathered together in the upper room. In Acts 2:41 we read that 3,000 became Christians in one day. So there was a church of at least 3,120, with twelve elders and no Jesus.

How could they be the church? How do we explain the awe? Of course we explain it by recognizing that Jesus really was there, even though He wasn't there. "I must go away, but I will come back to you," He had said. The presence of the Holy Spirit is the presence of Jesus. He does what Jesus does. He says what Jesus says. The Holy Spirit brings to our minds the things Jesus taught us. That is what Peter explains in his sermon at Pentecost.

By God's good grace to us the book of Acts goes a step further, in 2:42, and spells out four concrete things the church did. If you have been around the church of the Lord Jesus Christ for any length of time, you have heard these four activities talked about: the apostles' teaching, fellowship, the breaking of bread, and prayer. They encourage, on one hand, the worship of God's people and are, on the other hand, the expression of that worship as the people of God go out from their gathered times together.

Teaching

Worship always leads God's people to take the words of the apostles seriously—and the words of all the other writers of Scripture as well. It is not just the words that Peter and Paul spoke in the book of Acts, and later that Paul wrote in his letters, that teach the church. The whole of the Bible does that.

The Holy Spirit does not speak on His own. He speaks what He has heard the Master say. He is the Light by which we read Scripture, so He is the Source of our knowledge as He points us to Jesus. And He is the Light of our understanding, the illumination of what we read.

The apostles' teaching is Jesus' teaching. He teaches us through their words. When Jesus finishes teaching what we call the Sermon on the Mount, Matthew says that the people are astonished at the authority of His teaching. It is unlike anything they have ever heard (Matt. 7:28-29).

In John 7 the people marvel because Jesus says His own teaching is from God *and* that we will know it is from God when we obey it (v. 17). The self-authenticating truth of the Word of God comes home to our hearts only when it is true in our feet and our hands. Isn't that beautiful? Isn't that the church? The only way that the worship of Jesus is really going to sing in our hearts, the only way the beauty of Jesus is going to redound to the glory of His praise again and again in our lives is by our being obedient. Our hearts must worship, and our feet must run quickly to do the Savior's bidding, obeying His Word.

In Acts 5:28, the authorities condemn the apostles, saying, "We strictly charged you not to teach in [his] name, yet here you have filled

Jerusalem with your teaching." We cannot be filled with awe if we are not filled with the teaching of Jesus. There is no separation of worship from the Lord's Word. Worship revolves around the Lord's Word *always*. It is not just that the sermon is the longest part of worship—I don't know if sermons are supposed to be as long as they are; I don't know that the sermons in the early church were anything like the sermons that we hear today. The point is that the teaching of the truth of God's Word should bring a sense of awe.

Fellowship

The biblical word for fellowship is *koinonia*, which literally means "a sharing." The question should come to our minds, "What is it exactly that the apostles and the early church were sharing?" They were teaching the Lord's Word, and they were sharing that Word.

Second, we know that they shared in the breaking of the bread, which undoubtedly meant not only the communion meal but the meals that they shared in their homes, house to house, as it says in Acts 2.

Third, we also know that they shared their material wealth. Verse 44 says that they "had all things in common." They sold their possessions and shared the proceeds as any had need.

I am reluctant to limit this concept of "everything in common" as if I'm denying the importance of this sharing. But it is important to note that this was not a newly conceived social order, not Christian socialism or anything like it. It was temporary. We don't find this kind of sharing later in the book of Acts or anywhere else in the early church except in Jerusalem. But don't let those truths mitigate the impact of this verse: God's people always respond to a culture of greed by meeting the needs of the people in the church.

That is why deacons are so important in a church. The primary task of deacons is not to take care of a beautiful church building or to prepare the church budget but to lead God's people in the ministry of mercy. The gospel goes forward on two legs, always and everywhere: Word and deed, Word and mercy cannot be separated.

The Word and mercy were not separated in the ministry of Jesus. Every one of the Gospels has an opening statement about the ministry of Jesus. They say that He came to preach the gospel of the Kingdom, but also that He healed those who had any sickness.

Have you ever noticed how sometimes Jesus would preach the Word and not do anything merciful? And sometimes He would do something merciful but not preach the Word very much. Sometimes He would do both in a different order.

Modern-day evangelicals normally say, "Come and get saved, and Jesus is going to give you what you need." But Jesus does something different. He touches their lives. He heals them sometimes, and then He says, "Go, and do not sin anymore. Your sins have been forgiven."

This confuses us modern-day evangelicals who got off the hook about a hundred years ago by removing so-called social action from the message of the gospel. Today we continue to drive a wedge between two elements that were never intended to be divided—Word and deed. Perhaps we have lost much of what caused such great awe in the early church.

In the midst of the selfish culture of the ancient world, people were sharing what they possessed, and it was a way in which hearts and lives were changed. More than anything else, in the sharing of the Word, of their common meals, of their material wealth, their fellowship consisted of their sharing of Jesus. They knew Jesus together. They worshiped Him together, and then they talked about Him with one another and all over town. They did "good gossip" all over the city of Jerusalem about Jesus. Their common possession of Christ was central.

There was a common unity, a community. There were macro-communities meeting in the temple, praising God, and there were micro-communities meeting house to house. Acts 2 does not know anything about the individualistic approach to spirituality that is very common in our time. Today's evangelicals are like deep-sea divers who go down encased in heavy, deep-sea suits to protect them from the pressure several hundred feet below the surface. We walk around encased in protection with a lifeline to a common Source of life, Jesus. But frequently we have little communication with one another on the bottom of the ocean—except maybe an awkward wave at times. That is not a picture of the church.

The New Testament church is pictured again and again as *a family,* a family that loves one another in joy and trial. In 1 Timothy 3, the church is called God's household, and we are to call one another brothers and sisters and fathers and mothers. The church is intended to be a place where there is something magical about the way we care for one another. And that really does attract people.

One time my friend Doug Holladay and two friends, one of whom also spoke Spanish, were on a boat off the coast of Costa Rica. They were having a great time together, laughing and talking in English. They were three Christian brothers just enjoying one another. There was another fellow standing nearby just watching them. Finally he went up to the Spanish-speaking friend and spoke Spanish to him. They talked back and forth for a minute. Doug and the other friend asked, "What is he saying?" The Spanish-speaking member of the trio said, "This fellow doesn't know who we are, but he says that whatever it is that we are into, he wants to be a part of it." That is something of what the church should be.

Communion

As followers of Christ, there is an awe about who we are. It is a sense that we belong together. We love each other. That is why it is so important that on Sunday morning evangelical churches reflect that love in worship as well as in deed. Our family fellowship is most celebrated as we gather around the table for the Lord's Supper. The Lord's Supper is a sign and a seal. In recent years, I have come to believe more than ever before that it should be central to our worship.

In our church in Dallas we studied whether or not to observe the Lord's Supper at every single worship service, every single Sunday. We backed away from that for reasons that I think are acceptable. The question is, Do I believe, as a minister of the Word of God, that the sacrament is constitutive of Christian worship? I come close to saying it is, but I back away from it just enough, because I think there is enough example in the New Testament of variations of the theme. But I do believe the Lord's Supper is much more important than we evangelicals generally think it is.

It is a sign of the Lord's death—Jesus' body, broken for you, His blood shed for you. It is a sign of a believer's participation in the crucified Christ. Our union with Christ is symbolized in the union that we have as we partake of this meal, our communion with Him.

The Lord says, "Take, eat; this is my body" (Matt. 26:26). I don't back away from those words as I administer communion. I say, "Take, eat; this is the body of Christ." I know it is bread, and I am not getting confused along with others who mix that up, but the Lord Himself in His Word doesn't bother to go into a long explanation about why transubstantiation is wrong. He simply says, "Take, eat; this is my body, broken for you."

Prayer

When we read about prayer in Acts 1:14 and 2:42, it is all about "prayer together." There is probably no aspect of the church's worship or the Christian's life that is more talked about and yet more neglected.

The Puritan Thomas Goodwin pointed out that in our fallen

human nature we are actually allergic to God, and the closer we get to Him in prayer, the more the allergy starts to break out. That is the reason we pull away from God in prayer. That is why, when we know we should take that quiet fifteen minutes to pray, we find something else to do with that time.

It is not wrong to be reminded of a simple but sobering truth: Satan does not want us to pray, especially together. And just as Satan can tempt us to do wrong, he can also tempt us not to do right. The reason for Satan's allergy to prayer is twofold:

First, prayer releases the power of Christ's mighty acts into history and into the life of people. The very things that Peter talked about in his sermon—the ministry of Jesus Christ, His death, His resurrection, His exaltation, the things we call the gospel—have enormous power. The gospel is the power of God unto salvation. It is not just something that we believe once. It is not just a ticket to get into heaven. It is the power of God to change us. That means that the recitation and the application in our lives of these truths about Christ's ministry, His death, His resurrection, and His exaltation releases power to change us, our cities, and our world.

Second, prayer removes blockages to God's Kingdom work. Anyone who cares about Kingdom extension knows that God can and does alert us to blockages and gives us a sense of urgency about them. The spiritually sensitive among us will always help us see those strongholds of the strong man (see Matt. 12:29; 2 Cor. 10:4), which often take shape in terms of the idolatrous configurations of our heart.

A man cannot love and serve Jesus if he is visiting the wrong places on the Internet. That is a stronghold of the strong man. A man or a woman cannot worship and serve Jesus if he or she is worshiping at the altar of material success. A young person cannot worship Jesus if all he or she thinks about is success on the athletic field or in the classroom. These are strongholds of the strong man. Jesus says that only prayer, often with fasting, is strong enough to throw out the strong man (see Matt. 17:21 n.). Satan wants us to be allergic to that kind of praying.

John Piper describes prayer as a "wartime walkie-talkie," connecting the front lines with the supply troops. I love that image. We are out on the front lines, fighting a battle. We are the church militant, the army moving forward, and we need supplies from the back lines. Prayer is the walkie-talkie that tells the supply officer that we need those supplies and begs that they be brought forward. Piper goes on to urge his readers not to turn this wartime walkie-talkie into merely an "intercom" that connects the family room with the kitchen for relaying a request for something trivial like a glass of iced tea.[1] We demean prayer and the Lord Himself when we turn prayer into that which is intended to serve only our own comfort or our own ends.

Corporate prayer must not be just about our personal needs but must also be Kingdom-centered. This kind of prayer fills us with awe as we see God work. Awe is produced when the strongholds of the strong man are defeated. Awe is produced when God's people see the Kingdom advanced on our knees.

APPREHENSION OF THE BEAUTIFUL ONE

Worship is wanting to see Jesus Christ. It is wanting to see Him and love Him more than we want to see or love anything else. The implications of that kind of worship will always be worked out in the church, the Body of Christ, and then beyond the Body, so that everyone in the Body and outside of the Body has a sense of awe that something wonderful is going on that we can't control. The means by which this will happen are the means of grace: the apostles' teaching, the fellowship of God's people, the sacrament of holy communion, and our prayer, especially our prayer—Kingdom-centered, Kingdom-advancing prayer.

I want to say a word about the city. I don't care whether you think of the city as Dallas, Texas; Washington, D.C.; London, England; or whatever city or small town you are from—I think the city is intended to be changed by the worship of its churches and the obedient implications of that worship.

Apparently the city of Jerusalem actually rejoiced that the church was there, even though they persecuted it. That is an odd twist, yet we should expect no less. We will be persecuted at the same time that the very people who are planning our persecution are rejoicing at the fact that this thing called the church is there.

You remember that the Bible begins in a garden. Have you noticed that it ends in a city? We don't go back to the garden. Redemption is not redemption back to the beauty, bliss, simplicity, wonder, and loveliness of that garden, as great as it was. Redemption points us forward to the city of God, and the New Jerusalem is the picture of the new heavens and the new earth, where Jesus will be worshiped as the Lamb who is in the center of it all.

In the Bible, God never tells people to leave the wicked city, except when He is about to judge it, as He did when He commanded Lot and his family to leave Sodom. As bad as the city of Babel was, He didn't command people to leave it. He scattered them, yes, but to make new cities. God's people are to be a blessing in the city. They are to seek the welfare of the city. The church of the Lord Jesus Christ does not exist just *in* the city; it exists *for* the city, and there should be a great blessing that comes to the city because the people of God are there. When that happens, the city will be filled with awe, and some or many in that city will come to see the One who one day will be at the center of the New Jerusalem. They will join us and the elders and myriads of myriads who will gather around the throne and sing praise to the Lamb in the midst of the New Jerusalem.

Only with the church that worships and obeys that way has Jesus promised that the New Jerusalem will come. And only when everyone in the city continues to be filled with awe at us, will they come to understand who we truly are. We pray that then they will come to understand that we are filled with awe because we cannot take our eyes off the God who is beyond all praising—for He is too beautiful.

CHAPTER FIVE

How to Fire Your Imagination

Now he had to go through Samaria. So he came to a town in Samaria called Sychar, near the plot of ground Jacob had given to his son Joseph. Jacob's well was there, and Jesus, tired as he was from the journey, sat down by the well. It was about the sixth hour.

When a Samaritan woman came to draw water, Jesus said to her, "Will you give me a drink?" (His disciples had gone into the town to buy food.)

The Samaritan woman said to him, "You are a Jew and I am a Samaritan woman. How can you ask me for a drink?" (For Jews do not associate with Samaritans.)

Jesus answered her, "If you knew the gift of God and who it is that asks you for a drink, you would have asked him and he would have given you living water."

"Sir," the woman said, "you have nothing to draw with and the well is deep. Where can you get this living water? Are you greater than our father Jacob, who gave us the well and drank from it himself, as did also his sons and his flocks and herds?"

Jesus answered, "Everyone who drinks this water will be thirsty again, but whoever drinks the water I give him will never thirst. Indeed, the water I give him will become in him a spring of water welling up to eternal life."

The woman said to him, "Sir, give me this water so that I won't get thirsty and have to keep coming here to draw water."

He told her, "Go, call your husband and come back."

"I have no husband," she replied.

Jesus said to her, "You are right when you say you have no husband. The fact is, you have had five husbands, and the man you now have is not your husband. What you have just said is quite true."

"Sir," the woman said, "I can see that you are a prophet. Our fathers worshiped on this mountain, but you Jews claim that the place where we must worship is in Jerusalem."

Jesus declared, "Believe me, woman, a time is coming when you will worship the Father neither on this mountain nor in Jerusalem. You Samaritans worship what you do not know; we worship what we do know, for salvation is from the Jews. Yet a time is coming and has now come when the true worshipers will worship the Father in spirit and truth, for they are the kind of worshipers the Father seeks. God is spirit, and his worshipers must worship in spirit and in truth."

The woman said, "I know that Messiah" (called Christ) "is coming. When he comes, he will explain everything to us."

Then Jesus declared, "I who speak to you am he" (John 4:4-26, NIV).

THE IMAGINATION IS ONE of the most relevant and important subjects Christian people can discuss and ponder. What we load into our imaginations will determine the course of our lives. Put the wrong things in the imagination of our hearts, and inevitably wrong actions and unhappy living will result. Put the right things in, and we will discover a different way of living and thinking, a way that truly leads to what the Bible calls happy and blessed people.

So if it is very critical *what* we put in the imagination of our hearts, *how* do we put the right things in our imagination? How is it that our imagination is captured by what God says in His Word that it should be captured by?

I am a realist, and I know something of the world in which many Christians live and work and struggle day by day. I make it my business to find out about the ups and downs of members of our church. I know that this business called the Christian life is not easy all the time, and that it can be very difficult at times to keep in the imagination of our hearts the things that will motivate us to the life that we really want to lead. How do we fire up the imagination so that our hearts are fed with what God says should shape and mold our lives?

Like-minded people both before and since the Reformation have thought about this notion of shaping and molding the contours of our imaginations by what have been called the means of grace. The means of grace are defined as those things that help us get the right things into our hearts. As we noted in the last chapter, the means of grace are worship, Scripture, prayer, and fellowship with one another. Worship is really the primary means, the summary of them all.

SETTING THE STAGE

The meeting of Jesus and the Samaritan woman at the well, described in John 4, takes place as Jesus' popularity in Judea is increasing. His disciples are growing in number rapidly. In fact, when Jesus hears that His disciples are beginning to outnumber the disciples of John the Baptist, He decides to leave Judea and go to Galilee in order to prevent the precipitation of a crisis before the appropriate time.

A little geography is relevant here. For Jesus to get from Judea in the south to Galilee in the north, He had to walk through Samaria unless He went the long way around, east of the Jordan River—which Jews would actually do in order to avoid Samaria. But Jesus walked right up the middle of the land. He came to Sychar, which today is called the village of Ascar, near Nablus in the West Bank. In Genesis there is a reference to Jacob buying land in this vicinity, and while there is no reference to digging a well in Genesis, it would be clear that anyone who would buy land there would first seek to find water on it.

Jesus comes to a well. It had a wood or stone lip, on which Jesus sat. Literally, the text says that Jesus, being wearied from His journey, was "sitting thus" by the well. *Thus* is a reference to His weary state—dusty, thirsty, and hot from His travels.

When we vacation on the Outer Banks of North Carolina each summer, my family always does something special on one particular morning. We climb Jockey's Ridge, the largest natural sand dune on the East Coast of the United States. It is a huge mountain of sand.

Climbing it is fun, and it is hard. But we get the whole family up it. At the top the winds blow quite strongly, pushing sand and grit into our hair, eyes, and ears. By the time we come back down, we feel something like perhaps Jesus felt as He came to the well here at Sychar: hot, tired, gritty, badly in need of a drink of water.

John tells us that Jesus sits down at the sixth hour. That means noon, the heat of the day. It is remarkable that anyone besides Jesus is at the well at this time of day. He is traveling, and so it would be understandable that He would come to the well at that time. But most people, including the women who would come to the well for water, would usually come early in the morning or in the cool of the evening. The fact that this woman is here now, when other women would not be, is a hint of how she is perceived by her fellow villagers. She is avoiding them.

Jesus asks this woman for a drink. In that day it was not so unusual in itself for a man to ask a woman to draw water for him at a well. The difference is the real reason for Jesus' request. He intends, quite obviously, to engage this woman in conversation about more than just water. In fact, it is likely that He sends His disciples away to buy food so that He can be alone with her. Otherwise it seems a little unusual for twelve fellows to go off to buy groceries for thirteen people!

What is startling from this woman's perspective is that a Jew would speak to her, a Samaritan. (She knows Jesus is a Jew by His accent.) There was a history of great animosity between the Jews and the Samaritans. Samaria, along with all of northern Israel, was invaded by the Assyrians in 722 B.C. They were badly beaten, and most of the Israelite inhabitants were taken off in exile to distant cities. Only the very poor were allowed to remain.

Meanwhile, the Assyrians themselves moved into Israel. And in the region of Samaria they intermarried with the Israelite Jews. The Assyrian colonists found the place in awful shape, so they thought that perhaps they could improve the culture by getting right with the local god. They asked their king back in Assyria if it would be all right if they participated in Jewish worship. The result was an adulterated Judaism, a combination of Jewish and pagan worship. The Samaritan religion was a religion of convenience, a socially contrived religion that was disdained by the true Jews both to the north in Galilee and to the south in Judea. A couple of centuries later, when the Jews of southern Israel were rebuilding the temple in Jerusalem, the Samaritans asked if they could help, but the Jews said, "No, thank you." Out of jealousy the Samaritans said, "Well, if you are going to build your temple in Jerusalem, we'll build one of our own here in Samaria." So they built a temple on Mount Gerizim. This temple was burned by the Jews in 128 B.C., and relations between the Jews and the Samaritans worsened. By Jesus' time they were quite bitter.

THE LIVING WATER

This background helps us understand the woman's question in verse 9: "You are a Jew and I am a Samaritan woman. How can you ask me for a drink?" Then John adds parenthetically, "(For Jews do not associate with Samaritans.)" Jesus responds by saying something unexpected and curious: "If you knew the gift of God and who it is that asks you for a drink, you would have asked him and he would have given you living water" (v. 10, NIV).

Living water probably would have been recognized by this woman as a reference to flowing or bubbling water, water from a spring as opposed to stagnant water. But it was also, in light of the well being there, a reference to the deeper water of the well. The deeper water was better, and it was spoken of as the living water. Perhaps this accounts for the woman's response: "Sir, . . . you have nothing to draw with and the well is deep. Where can you get this living water?" (v. 11, NIV).

There is more in her response than just an interesting discussion about how one is to dig deep for the best water. It is clear that she is realizing that Jesus is calling attention to Himself. The *sir* here is a term of respect, but does it not also distance her from Jesus? She begins to realize that Jesus is making some claim. And so she asks, "Are you greater than our father Jacob, who gave us the well and drank from it himself?" (v. 12, NIV). She is beginning to think about the importance of this stranger.

Jesus responds by contrasting the temporary benefit of drinking the water that would be drawn from the well, with the permanent benefit of receiving water from Him. "Everyone who drinks this water will be thirsty again," Jesus said. "But whoever drinks the water I give him will never thirst. Indeed, the water I give him will become in him a spring of water welling up to eternal life" (vv. 4:13-14, NIV).

Jesus plays upon a notion that would be familiar to this woman—living water—and uses that to talk about a living water that is deeper, purer, truer, and more satisfying than any physical water could be. Jesus is saying that the living water He provides becomes a vigorous stream in those who drink of it. The life that Jesus gives is no stagnant thing. He wants her to realize that when He gives life, it is rich and abundant. Later in His ministry, Jesus stands up in the midst of the great feast in Jerusalem and cries out, "If anyone is thirsty, let him come to me and drink. Whoever believes in me, as the Scripture has said, streams of living water will flow from within him" (John 7:37-38, NIV). By this "he meant the Spirit, whom those who believed in him were later to receive" (v. 39, NIV). The water that Jesus gives is the Holy Spirit, who comes to our spirits and makes us aware of who we are becoming as new people in and through Christ. The Holy Spirit is that water of life that takes away the deepest of thirsts.

It is obvious that the power and the conviction of Jesus' own words about this living water impresses the woman. She says, "Sir, give me this water so that I won't get thirsty and have to keep coming here to draw water" (John 4:15, NIV). She is partially there, but she is still thinking in terms of literal, physical water. She thinks how good it would be to have this magic water so that she wouldn't have to lug pitchers out to the well while avoiding the scorn of other women in the community. She doesn't understand yet, but she is hooked.

THE PLACE OF WORSHIP

Then Jesus surprises her by saying, "Go, call your husband and come back" (v. 16, NIV). Knowing what we know about this woman and what Jesus apparently knew about her, it seems rather impolite of Him to introduce into this present conversation the uncomfortable subject of this woman's marital status. Is He being too blunt? Bluntness about our thirst, about the emptiness in our hearts, about our sin is sometimes necessary if we are to learn how to drink the water that truly takes away the thirst.

"I have no husband," the woman replies. It is a very abrupt answer. In the original language it is only three words. Perhaps she is hoping that Jesus will assume she is a widow or that she never married. While it is technically true that she has no husband, that is not the full truth. Jesus then tells her the truth: she has had five husbands, and the man she is now living with is not legally her husband at all.

"Sir," the woman says, "I can see that you are a prophet. Our fathers worshiped on this mountain, but you Jews claim that the place where we must worship is in Jerusalem" (vv. 19-20, NIV). She seems to change the subject, attempting to move the discussion from herself and her needs to a religiously abstract topic about the proper location of worship, a theoretical discussion about the right place for a temple to exist. She is like us, isn't she? When the searchlight of God's penetrating power begins to reckon with the truth of what is in our own hearts, all of a sudden we get very interested in the rapture or predestination.

No doubt this woman's questions hold interest for her, as our questions do for us. But the timing for these questions is suspicious! If I were Jesus, I would say, "Now, look here, let's get back to the subject." But Jesus sees how the question is really more to the point than the woman may think. Just as she wants to reduce the living water that God gives to something tangible, she wants to simplify her religious life by confining it to a specific location.

If we can deal with God in a certain place and at a certain time, then the implication is that we are free to live the rest of our lives the way we want to. If God is in the church building where we worship and attend Sunday school and committee meetings—but only in the church building—we can live the rest of our lives beyond those walls as we please.

Jesus declares, "Believe me, woman, a time is coming when you will worship the Father neither on this mountain nor in Jerusalem" (v. 21, NIV). The key religious debate between the Jews and the Samaritans turns out to be a smokescreen. The issue is not whether worship takes place in a high school auditorium or in a sanctuary or in a tent. Jesus says the issue is how worship takes place. He proclaims, "Yet a time is coming and has now come when the true worshipers will worship the Father in spirit and truth, for they are the kind of worshipers the Father seeks. God is spirit, and his worshipers must worship in spirit and in truth" (vv. 23-24, NIV).

Jesus is saying that the issue is not how often or where you worship. The issue is what kind of heart you bring to worship. "The issue, oh, Samaritan woman," Jesus says, "is that my being the Messiah changes the location of worship from an exterior physical place to an interior place of the Spirit."

WORSHIPING IN SPIRIT

Because God is spirit, physical worship in some physical place, however right that place is, is not enough. Because God is spirit, real worship is spiritual; that is, it proceeds from our spirits, from our inner beings. *Spirit* here is rightly understood as a synonym for *heart,* or one's inner being, rather than as a reference to the Holy Spirit.

The New Testament is largely indifferent about the exterior forms of worship. It doesn't say we must worship God in a cathedral or use a certain liturgy or sing certain hymns or songs. It doesn't say whether the minister has to wear a robe or can preach in an open collar. None of that seems very important in the New Testament. But the New Testament *is* passionate about the inner attitude we bring to our worship. To worship God in spirit is to worship in the sincerity and earnestness of our hearts. That is what God is concerned about. He is not concerned about the exterior forms. He is concerned about the reality of genuine worship in our hearts. So to worship God in spirit is to genuinely worship, not to play with it or to play at it or to go through the motions or just to stand up, sit down, lean to the left, lean to the right.

Worship is not a matter of sitting on the well and discussing in an abstract way the different qualities of water that come from different depths in the well. No, worship is to drink the water. Worship is to take of the water that is given to us and to be filled by it so that our thirst is quenched. The worshipers that Jesus wants, that the Father seeks, are worshipers who worship out of their spirit.

Worshiping in Truth

They are also worshipers, Jesus says, who worship in truth. Truth and spirit, spirit and truth. To worship God in truth is to worship the God who is truly there, not the God of our projection; not the God that we want to be there, but the God of truth. How do we know who the God of truth is? From the Bible. And that is why true worship will always be worship that is structured by, oriented around, defined by, and originating from the Scriptures. We don't worship the Book, but the Book brings us the One whom we worship in truth.

The Scriptures tell us who He is in truth; therefore, preaching must always be out of the Scriptures, not out of the preacher's mind, not out of the newspaper that week, not out of what the preacher made up in the shower that morning. If you haven't done so already, find a church where the preaching of the Word is central, and you will be worshiping in truth because you will be worshiping the true God.

To worship in truth means not only do we worship the true God, but we worship God as we truly are. So we come with our five husbands and our ambition and our greed and our sensuality and our envy and our covetousness. We don't hide behind religious masks. Maybe we don't turn to the person in the pew behind us whom we have just met and confess every sin we've ever committed, but we do speak honestly to God. We cannot hide from God in worship. It is preposterous to even think we can. God knows us through and through, and He wants real worship from a true heart that worships Him as He truly is.

What kind of worshipers does God seek? Those who worship Him not just at certain times and not just in certain places and certainly not lackadaisically and not yawning their way through a worship service. Take a cold shower before you go to worship if you need to. But wake up. Jog three miles if you have to. But go to worship awake, because God is forever awake, and He is seeking those whose hearts are awake and alive in spirit and truth to worship Him. We don't go with plastic smiles but in truth, with an earnest desire to worship Him in spirit.

HEAT AND LIGHT

Spirit and truth belong together. Spirit or emotion without truth is excitement without meaning. Truth without spirit is dry as dust. Both are inadequate alone. God wants holy feelings—what Jonathan Edwards called "holy affection"—hearts that are aflame, imaginations that have come alive with the reality of the God who is alive. He doesn't want play-acting in worship. He wants the real thing.

The Bible demands that our imagination be fired in worship. Just look at the book of Psalms. Open to any worship psalm. What does the book of Psalms call for in worship? It calls for being stopped cold, or we might say better, being stopped hot by the holiness of God. It calls for awe, or what we might rightly call fear. It calls for humbleness. It calls for longing for God. It calls for laughing. It calls for weeping. It calls for proclaiming. It calls for silence. It calls for clapping, not to approve a performance but to make a loud noise joyfully before God.

As we said earlier, worship is not a duty—not primarily. A duty is something we think about performing as we should. Too much emphasis upon worship as a duty turns it to legalism, which God hates in worship more than He hates almost anything else.

But isn't duty a noble thing? Surely we honor those we dutifully serve. Yes, but we must understand that honor without heart, duty without desire, truth without spirit is *subnormal* for the Christian life, and it quickly turns to legalism, to worship of the lips but not of the heart. The worship that God wants is the worship of a freed imagination, from hearts that can't help themselves, as lovers can't help praising one another.

Jonathan Edwards talked about spirit and truth as heat and light. Heat is the warmth of spirit, the fervency of heart. Truth is the light that is needed to see, to illuminate. In 1744 Edwards preached a sermon about the dangers of pitting either heat or light against the other. He said, "If a minister has light without heat, he entertains his hearers with learned discourses but without the power of godliness. And he will not be able thereby to reach their souls. But if, on the other hand, he be driven on with the fierce and intemperate zeal and a vehement heat without light, he will be likely to kindle the unhallowed flame in his people to fire their corrupt passions and affections, but will make them never the better nor lead them a step toward heaven but drive them apace the other way."[1]

Heat without light is sentimentality. Or worse, it is corruptible passion.

Light without heat may appeal to the logic, but it will not feed the soul.

The sacraments are so important because they portray the truth of the gospel, and its visual portrayal before us kindles our imagination. Worship gives heat and light to our heart's imagination. Worship fills our imaginations with truth about God and with warmth from God. So worship must be hot to the touch and light to the eyes. It must warm our hearts and also lead us to "Aha's" of recognition about who God is and who we are.

Because our worship is so often weak and because we could not create a spark, let alone a fire, from our own imaginations, the Father seeks out our hearts. He kindles there a blaze of worship. The Father is the Great Seeker for worshipers. Though we are created for worship, too often we are distracted from the real thing. The Father keeps seeking us and keeps firing our imaginations with His white, hot, holy flame so that we are reminded that where there is heat and light—where we can be warm and full of truth—in that place we know Jesus is the joy of loving hearts. Only Jesus Christ ignites our imaginations. The fireplace is the place of worship, and His fire will be hot.

Chapter Six

Drawing Near

Therefore, brothers, since we have confidence to enter the holy places by the blood of Jesus, by the new and living way that he opened for us through the curtain, that is, through his flesh, and since we have a great priest over the house of God, let us draw near with a true heart in full assurance of faith, with our hearts sprinkled clean from an evil conscience and our bodies washed with pure water. Let us hold fast the confession of our hope without wavering, for he who promised is faithful. And let us consider how to stir up one another to love and good works, not neglecting to meet together, as is the habit of some, but encouraging one another, and all the more as you see the Day drawing near (Heb. 10:19-25).

For you have not come to what may be touched, a blazing fire and darkness and gloom and a tempest and the sound of a trumpet and a voice whose words made the hearers beg that no further messages be spoken to them. For they could not endure the order that was given, "If even a beast touches the mountain, it shall be stoned." Indeed, so terrifying was the sight that Moses said, "I tremble with fear." But you have come to Mount Zion and to the city of the living God, the heavenly Jerusalem, and to innumerable angels in festal gathering, and to the assembly of the firstborn who are enrolled in heaven, and to God, the judge of all, and to the spirits of the righteous made perfect, and to Jesus, the mediator of a new covenant, and to the sprinkled blood that speaks a better word than the blood of Abel. See that you do not refuse him who is speaking. For if they did not escape when they refused him who warned them on earth, much less will we escape if we reject him who warns from heaven (Heb. 12:18-25).

HAVE YOU EVER HAD the experience of being attracted to and fearful of someone at the same time? If you think about it, you would

probably say, "Of course!" Sometime in your life there has been someone whom you really admired and perhaps wanted to get close to.
Maybe you have greatly admired an older person in your business
arena, one you wanted to have as a mentor or a friend, but something caused you apprehension about getting too close; something held
you back, maybe a little fear or uncertainty as to whether or not you
would be well received. Both attraction and fear are often elements
that characterize some of our very real and human relationships.

A number of years ago when my son Chris was about ten years
old, he and I were invited to attend the Fiesta Bowl. That year happened to be the year when the national college football championship
would be determined there, so we got to see the two best teams in
the country play. We were the very privileged guests of a good friend
who had a private box and passes to get us into all the right places.
(It was very impressive.)

As Chris and I waited for an elevator to the skybox, I looked
around and saw people who did not represent the usual crowd at a
football game. I recognized some well-known personalities, and then
I saw one person in particular whom I couldn't help but notice—
Charles Barkley, the basketball player. I thought, "This is an oppor-
tunity that I don't want to miss because Chris admires Charles
Barkley very much." I wanted to capture the moment, and I had to
move quickly because people were proceeding to the elevators. So I
immediately said, "Hello, Charles!"

He looked at me as if to say, "Do I know you?" or "Am I supposed to know you?" I knew that in just another second he would
realize that he didn't know me at all and would turn away. So before
he could do that, I blurted, "Charles, say hello to my son Chris."

And Charles Barkley, much to his credit, did not miss a beat. He
stuck out his hand, took Chris's hand, shook it, and said, "Hi, Chris,
it's nice to meet you."

Chris stared into Barkley's eyes and stuttered, "Uh, uh, uh."

Indeed, we nearly had to pick Chris up off the floor. He couldn't believe it. He didn't want to ever wash his hand—a hand, he must have thought, that would thenceforth shoot the perfect jump shot! That combination of attraction and fear is what Chris was feeling, particularly since Charles Barkley was a bigger-than-life figure and not known for his gentle ways, at least on the basketball court!

Approaching the Mountain

The author of Hebrews says that when we draw near to God in worship, it is completely legitimate that we should have this same combination of attraction and fear, particularly if we understand what the Old Testament teaches us about the nature of worship. That is the background of the author's teaching in Hebrews 10 and 12. If we understand the Old Testament at all, we should find ourselves caught in the ambivalence of great attraction to God, wanting to be in His presence and worship Him, yet, at the same time, having a legitimate fear that would cause us to back away.

Hebrews 12:18 tells us that in worship we have come to a mountain. It speaks of the Old Testament people of God coming to a mountain that cannot be touched, and to a burning fire, darkness, gloom, and storm. Is that the way you think about coming to worship God—in terms of darkness and storm and ferocious sound? Probably not, but the Old Testament people of God thought just that way!

Read Exodus 19. There you will capture the flavor of what it was like for the Israelites to think about drawing near to God and worshiping Him. Feel the ambivalence that they undoubtedly had in their heads and hearts as they thought about their attraction to God on the one hand and yet their legitimate fear of coming too close to Him on the other.

In Exodus 19:12-13, God Himself speaks to Moses about the place where they are meeting together, Mount Sinai: "And you shall set limits for the people all around, saying, 'Take care not to go up into the mountain or touch the edge of it. Whoever touches the mountain shall be put to death. No hand shall touch him, but he shall be stoned or shot; whether beast or man, he shall not live.' When the trumpet sounds a long blast, they shall come up to the mountain."

Now look at verses 16 and following:

> On the morning of the third day there were thunders and lightnings and a thick cloud on the mountain and a very loud trumpet blast, so that all the people in the camp trembled. Then Moses brought the people out of the camp to meet God, and they took their stand at the foot of the mountain. Now Mount Sinai was wrapped in smoke because the LORD had descended on it in fire. The smoke of it went up like the smoke of a kiln, and the whole mountain trembled greatly. And as the sound of the trumpet grew louder and louder, Moses spoke, and God answered him in thunder. The LORD came down on Mount Sinai, to the top of the mountain. And the LORD called Moses to the top of the mountain, and Moses went up.
>
> And the LORD said to Moses, "Go down and warn the people, lest they break through to the LORD to look [literally *to gaze,* as if to gaze on God] and many of them perish. Also let the priests who come near to the LORD consecrate themselves, lest the LORD break out against them." And Moses said to the LORD, "The people cannot come up to Mount Sinai, for you yourself warned us, saying, 'Set limits around the mountain and consecrate it.'" And the LORD said to him, "Go down, and come up bringing Aaron with you. But do not let the priests and the people break through to come up to the LORD, lest he break out against them" (Ex. 19:16-24).

And then we read in Exodus 20:18-19, "Now when all the people saw the thunder and the flashes of lightning and the sound of the trumpet and the mountain smoking, the people were afraid and trembled, and they stood far off and said to Moses, 'You speak to us, and we will listen; but do not let God speak to us, lest we die.'"

Now this is ambivalence in worship! This is wanting to go up the mountain and be in the presence of God. But God also sees the arrogance of the people. Their desire to march into His presence by force reveals a heart attitude that is altogether too overconfident before Him. That is why He commands them not to come, lest they gaze at Him.

The word *gaze* implies seeking control of what they are looking at as they take it into account. The Lord is telling Moses not to let the people come if they do so arrogantly, without thinking, without awe. God expects that there should be great ambivalence in the hearts of those who come to worship Him.

Drawing near to God in the Old Testament is not accompanied by soft organ music or the sweet singing of, "Softly and tenderly Jesus is calling." No, the Old Testament is saying, "Do you really know who you are dealing with here?" This God is not a pushover. This God is not a grandfather in the sky. He does not wink at our wrong-doing. It is not His job to answer our prayers and to bless us. This God is a God who is so pure that the only way we can describe Him is as a consuming fire (Heb. 12:29). So how do we draw near to this God? This is a huge problem in the Old Testament, perhaps *the* problem of the whole Old Testament.

CONFIDENCE OR BRAVADO?

In light of what we read in Exodus and Hebrews, how can we saunter into God's presence? How can we come for two minutes of private prayer a day or sixty minutes of public worship a week? How can we come and think that we can have a nice chat and be warmed in our hearts, and then leave? Is it confidence, or is it unwarranted bravado to go in and be with such a God?

Live in the ambivalence of this reality for just a moment. Get a feel for what it means to come into the presence of God, to draw near to Him. In the Old Testament it is not something that one would do lightly or casually, skipping into His presence with a bouncy spring in one's step, as if to say, "Oh, God has nothing else on His mind this day but to just say hello to me." That is not the Old Testament way of thinking, even if it is very much a contemporary way of thinking about God.

The answer to the question, "How do you draw near to this kind of God?" must first be: "Change your view of God." But you resist, saying that the view of God that I have just described is absolutely too ferocious. Some would say, "That is the God of the Old Testament. I believe in the God of the New Testament."

I have some news for you: it is one and the same God in the Old and New Testaments.

Nevertheless, you say, "That God is just too much. I want a God who is warm and fuzzy. I want a God like James Van Praagh's God." Have you heard of Van Praagh? In a review of his book entitled *Talking to Heaven,* he is described as beyond New Age.[1] This former screenwriter and stagehand in Hollywood has taken up a very personal relationship, not only with one he calls God, but also with all kinds of spirits—those who have gone on before us, those who have already died. Van Praagh says that he can bring God to you through his midnight-blue eyes.

Van Praagh says that people will be able to experience a benevolent and kind god, a god who offers advice and jokes and opinions on a wide range of subjects but has no commandments. For this god, sex is wonderful and fun for everyone, and everyone, even Hitler, gets to go to heaven. There is a promise of eternal life without the necessity of believing anything beyond the grasp of an average dog or cat. And speaking of pets, he believes that he can help us renew our friendship with our lost pets. Now this may sound bizarre, but this book was number one on *The New York Times* best-seller list in 1998. And Van Praagh's type of thinking has only become more widespread since then.

A history professor at Cornell University, R. Laurence Moore, says that this is actually a very familiar theme in American spirituality, going back at least to the Transcendentalists of the nineteenth century. Thoreau, Emerson, and Van Praagh all expound the same fool-ish, repetitive ideas—ideas that go down easily. That is what we want—a god who goes down easily. [2] We want a god who is fluff and warmth and merriment and lightness. We don't want thunder or smoke or fire. We don't want a God who, if He spoke, might strike us dead—or save us completely from a death He says we deserve!

Jerry Adler, the author of an article on Van Praagh, ends his piece this way: "I don't think I learned much about heaven from Van Praagh. But he did show me this: how eager each of us is to find some measure of transcendence as we make our lonely ways through this world of grief."[3] God is merely *transcendence* here, a transcen-dent other whom we want to help us make sense of our poor lives, but on our own terms.

HOW TO DRAW NEAR

The answer in our Bible, and particularly in the book of Hebrews, to how we can come to God is far richer and far more deserving of our thought and attention than the answers we find in best-sellers. Hebrews says that we can draw near to God, not because our pets are telling us through Mr. Van Praagh how to be happier people, but because of the gospel's power to change our standing before this awesome God.

Look at Hebrews 10:19-22 again: "Therefore, brothers, since we have confidence to enter the holy places by the blood of Jesus, by the new and living way that he opened for us through the curtain, that is, through his flesh, and since we have a great priest over the house of God, let us draw near . . ." Hebrews proclaims that we can come boldly into the very place where, at Sinai, people would have been scorched to death!

How and why can we do so? "Therefore, brothers . . ." What is the *therefore* there for? Look back at verses 10-11 (NIV): "And by that will, we have been made holy through the sacrifice of the body of Jesus Christ once for all. Day after day every priest stands and performs his religious duties; again and again he offers the same sacrifices, which can never take away sins."

The whole point of the sacrificial system in the Old Testament was to show us that no matter how many times a sacrifice was made, it could never take away sins, never complete the job for which it was intended. If the priest sacrificed for sins in the morning, he would have to go back and do it again that afternoon and again that night. And then he would have to start over the next day, because once was never enough; there were too many sins, too many things going on in heads and hearts every day. Sin was and is who we are—all that we are, not just what we do. The whole person who stood before this holy God *couldn't stand before this holy God*. We needed instead the once-and-for-all sacrifice.

Verses 12-14 state the result of this sacrifice: "But when Christ had offered for all time a single sacrifice for sins, he sat down at the right hand of God, waiting from that time until his enemies should be made a footstool for his feet. For by a single offering he has perfected for all time those who are being sanctified." There are two alternatives: either human beings will be a footstool for the Lord, or they will be made perfect with the holiness of Christ Himself.

If this, then, is what it means to draw near by the blood of Jesus, by the once-and-for-all sacrifice that allows us to enter into the holy place, this is what we must understand worship is. Worship is not coming together to sing a couple of hymns, to hear a beautiful choir, and to hear some inspiring thoughts. No, worship is a drawing near to the place we are forbidden to come. The only way in is to come bearing the merit, the righteousness, the work of the shed blood of Jesus, our Savior.

That is the only garment that you can wear to worship. It doesn't matter how nicely you dress for church. It doesn't matter whether the men wear ties or not, whether the women wear skirts or pants. As a minister of the gospel, I care much more about the garment that the *souls* of my flock are wearing than whether or not they wear a tie or a skirt.

The gospel is a better hope by which we draw near to God. Because of the ongoing intercessory prayers of Jesus, Christians can draw near to God. Hebrews 4:16 tells us that because of Jesus Christ, our High Priest, we can draw near to God in confidence. And Hebrews 10:22 says we can draw near with a sincere heart, with full assurance. The fear part of the equation is changed. Now there is enormous attraction.

Along with the attraction, there is also a metamorphosis of this fear. In a sense, it doesn't completely go away, because if we understand who this awesome God is, we will never come casually to Him. But fear is replaced with confidence. We come now confidently, respectfully, awe-fully, full of wonder—yes, full of fear in that sense. However, we come with confidence because of the blood of Christ, which has opened us to a new and better way.

Usually on Sunday mornings at the church I pastor, a procession of the choir comes down the middle aisle during the opening hymn. It is a reenactment of entering in, of the truth that we have the privilege of entering into the *sanctus*, the sanctuary—not a room, but the holy place of the assembly of God's people.

The holy place is *us*, if I could put it that way. That is so remarkable! In the Old Testament we could not have gone near the holy place. Now we *are* the holy place. Why?

Look at Hebrews 10:22: "Let us draw near with a true heart in full assurance of faith, with our hearts sprinkled clean from an evil conscience and our bodies washed with pure water." There is a connection here between the sprinkled water of baptism and the blood that was sprinkled on the ark of the covenant in the Old Testament temple and tabernacle, as if to pave the way into the presence of

God. So when Presbyterians and several other denominations baptize people by sprinkling, they are symbolizing that sprinkled blood of the Perfect Lamb—ultimately, the only blood that will allow us to enter into the holy place.

WHY WORSHIP?

The writer of Hebrews says in 10:23-25, "Let us hold fast the confession of our hope without wavering, for he who promised is faithful. And let us consider how to stir up one another to love and good works, not neglecting to meet together, as is the habit of some, but encouraging one another, and all the more as you see the Day drawing near."

It is the Day of Judgment that is drawing near. There is going to be an end to history. There will be a huge consummation, when all earthly worship as we know it will be over, and there will be a new heaven, a new earth, and a new reality. But until that day comes, do not stop gathering together to worship as God's people.

Those verses are often taken as verses commending fellowship, but actually, they commend worship. If we are wearing the garments of Christ's righteousness, worship is our deepest and truest identity. It is who we are, and it is not an optional extra that we do casually for an hour a week.

When I board one of those huge 767 or 777 airplanes for a flight, I think about the pilot up in the cabin and how I am putting a lot of trust in that guy. One of the most significant things that we have to trust him for is the landing. (A landing of a big airplane is really a controlled crash. That's all it is!) The first issue is, does the pilot have *access* to that airstrip? If he doesn't have clear access to it, if there are other planes in the way, on the ground or in the air, we are in trouble! The issue is access. If we do not have clear access, then we will crash and burn.

If we do not have clear access into the holy place of God's presence, and if we saunter in without making sure that the access has been made for us by the Holy One Himself, by Jesus Christ, then we will crash and burn. I promise you the Lord will not forever tolerate our casual attitude about worship. Instead we come in the name of the Righteous One and by His merit.

A New Mountain

Without the right access, we could never get there. But with the access provided by Jesus Christ, we can come not to Mount Sinai, the place of fire, burning, and thunder, but to a different mountain—Mount Zion. Look at Hebrews 12:22-24: "But you have come to Mount Zion and to the city of the living God, the heavenly Jerusalem, and to innumerable angels in festal gathering, and to the assembly of the firstborn who are enrolled in heaven, and to God, the judge of all, and to the spirits of the righteous made perfect, and to Jesus, the mediator of a new covenant, and to the sprinkled blood that speaks a better word than the blood of Abel."

Mount Sinai was the place where God's anger burned when the people were worshiping the image of a calf. Mount Sinai was the place where the Law was given, the mirror to be held up to our hearts, revealing what is there. The Law is the reason why we tremble with fear as Moses did. The Law is where we understand what it means to come to a holy God and to fear going in to Him. But the new and better way that turns fear into confidence is not given at Mount Sinai. It is given at Mount Zion.

Mount Zion is often the name for the city of Jerusalem in Scripture. Sometimes it is used synonymously for Jerusalem. Most specifically, however, it is the part of Jerusalem upon which the temple was built. It is where sacrifices for sins were offered.

Back in Genesis, before the city of Jerusalem existed, Mount Zion was called Mount Moriah. Remember what happened on Mount Moriah? Abraham took his son up to the top of Mount

Moriah and prepared to sacrifice him there. At the last moment, God spoke and said, "No," and provided a substitute.

Then the temple was built on Mount Zion, and the people of God would go there, and the high priest would tremble as he approached the altar. He would provide there the sacrifice that was looking forward to the yet-greater Sacrifice. Then on that very same place, Mount Zion/Mount Moriah, just a few yards away from where the temple was built, Jesus hung on the Cross. In that place God put His Son in the sacrificial place that you and I deserve.

He says now that we can worship here, we can come to Mount Zion, the place of the once-and-for-all Sacrifice, where the blood of Jesus was sprinkled. As His body was torn on Mount Zion, the veil in the temple was torn apart as well, and entrance to the Most Holy Place opened to those for whom He died. We can enter with full confidence and assurance because our consciences have been cleansed. And we come to Mount Zion, which is not just the city of ancient Jerusalem, but the focus of a new and heavenly Jerusalem.

THE JOYFUL ASSEMBLY

I have had the privilege of visiting Jerusalem a couple of times in my life, but Jerusalem is not where the action is. The action is in the worshiping church. We are the New Jerusalem. We are the people of God. We are the new Mount Zion. We are the ones in whom the Spirit of the Living Christ who died for us dwells. And that means we are the worshiping assembly of God's people.

We have come to Mount Zion, to the church of the firstborn, the church of joyful assembly of names written in heaven; to God, the Judge of all men; to Jesus, the Mediator. It is awe-some, literally full of awe, that when the Body of Christ gathers in a room, it is in the presence of the very God. And in the presence of the very God, even though we do not see them with physical eyes, we nevertheless have angels gathering with us—myriads and myriads of them. They are unseen, but there.

Or even better, *we* are there with *them*. There is a wonderful true transcendence in Christian worship, for not only are the angels there, but also the spirits of people declared righteous with the righteousness of Christ, who are now being made perfect. They are all there, and it is more permanent than anything we see—things that will one day be destroyed.

It is not too much to say they are all there. Your saintly grandmother who prayed for you, your dear friend you lost recently, the saints of other generations, the ones whose names we recognize—Augustine, Bernard of Clairvaux, Luther—and ones whose names we don't recognize but whose names are written in the Book of Life. They are there together with Eve; Moses; and Rebecca, who deceived her husband; and David the great king who was also a great sinner; Ruth; and Rahab the former prostitute—we are all there with them. We have come to Mount Zion, to the city of the Living God, to join in festal assembly—the happy gathering of God's people. We proceed into the Most Holy Place, where more present than anyone else is the Lamb of God, the precious Lamb of God who is at one and the same time the Priest, the Sacrifice, and the One who is worthy of our adoration and praise.

In that place there is a lot of music. In that place we see the Lamb wearing many crowns. In that place we join our voices with those who have gone before and who will come after in the communion of saints. And in that place there is one of two alternatives for everyone who is there. Hebrews 12:25 warns, "See that you do not refuse him who is speaking." And Hebrews 12:28 commands, "Therefore let us be grateful for receiving a kingdom that cannot be shaken, and thus let us offer to God acceptable worship, with reverence and awe." The first alternative is to refuse Him who speaks; the second alternative is to worship Him with reverence and awe.

If you refuse Him, then the Lord remains on Mount Sinai, unapproachable. And if you try to approach Him in your own way, refusing His way through the blood of Jesus, you will burn with fire. But if you come by way of the blood of Christ, if you come not to Mount Sinai but to Mount Zion, then you come as one whose soul will be made alive and full of life in the very presence of God and will join the grand, joyful assembly of saints and angels now and for all eternity. That is what you were made for.

What Is Worship?
An Interview with Skip Ryan

Q: What constitutes worship?

A: Most importantly, I think that the presence of God constitutes worship. It is not a human endeavor, but one that is inspired by the presence of the Lord Himself. When people gather for worship, it is fundamentally an assembling of God's people, the fellowship of the Holy Spirit. And God is the most important Person present. Frequently, during the invocation (or what we call the Prayer of Adoration) I will say things that will help people remember that.

The primary activity during worship is listening to and speaking to the Lord, not only in the proclamation of the Word but in the hymns and other elements of the worship service. We don't just hear Him through His Word; the whole environment speaks of His presence.

God's presence is the beginning point for biblical worship; in the Old Testament, where God is present, there worship takes place. Dignity and awe and solemnity are very appropriate in His presence. There are times in worship when we should be struck dumb, when clapping hands and shouting would be inappropriate, because at times we need to be silent before the Lord.

The assembly of God's people is the place of God's worship—

not the building. In the invocational prayer we are calling upon the Lord to be among His people, to do as He promised and constitute us as a worshiping assembly of His people.

Q: You have said there are some inadequate models of worship. What are they?

A: First, worship is not simply *instruction*. We should not see the worship service only in terms of the sermon, which is accompanied by a few "extras" like the offering and some hymns. To avoid this tendency, at times we may rearrange the order so the sermon is not the climax of worship.

Second, worship is not a *training center*. The worship service is not the time to train the congregation in evangelism, visitation, or discipleship. The emphasis in worship is on being, not doing. We may indeed learn how to do something; but we come first to learn that we are the Lord's people and that our primary purpose is to glorify Him and enjoy Him forever.

Third, the worship service is not simply *fellowship*. Surely fellowship takes place in worship, but the primary reason for being there is not horizontal; it is vertical. If the strongest feeling you have after a worship service is that you have been in the presence of other people, then perhaps you have not been in the presence of the Lord.

The purpose of worship is also not *evangelism*. Gearing a worship service primarily to the unchurched, in my opinion, is not worship. It may be an evangelism meeting, which is good, but it is not worship. Dr. Edmund Clowney talks of "doxological evangelism," which means as we praise God and worship Him, people are drawn to Him and are converted. It is true. I have seen people become Christians in our morning worship services, not because we directed the service evangelistically, but because they sensed a reality that they had never experienced before.

Finally, we should not see the worship service as *vision-building time* for the church. Using the service to promote the new building or new programs will cause you to end up with something less than worship.

Q: You advocate providing opportunities for people to participate in worship, not merely watch. How is this done?

A: There needs to be a balance between form and freedom (or spontaneity), between structure and liturgy, between formality and informality. I think we should use all the liturgical forms—creeds, liturgical prayers, and responsive readings, particularly the Psalms. But a worship service should also have pockets of freedom and spontaneity within the liturgy. These pockets of spontaneity—usually in the form of music, sharing, or praying—are the freedom within the form. The key is not to overly calculate some blend. The key is to focus on the presence of the Lord Jesus and let those who are worshiping worship in spirit and in truth. This means they must really worship and not just play at it.

Q: Where do you think that contemporary elements like drama fit in a worship service?

A: I think the worship service *is* drama, and we all (congregants and leaders) participate in it. I try to work that out in worship by moving around; I start out behind the Lord's table, move to the front for another part of the service, then later move to the pulpit to preach. Also, I think we should use all the beautiful instrumentation we can. The Psalms give us many examples of the music and drama of worship.

Celebrating the Lord's Supper is also part of the drama of worship; the Lord's Supper is the demonstration—the drama—of the gospel. I think pastors should make much more of the rightful place of the dramatic portrayal of the Lord's Supper than we do.

We derive spiritual benefit from the Lord's Supper, but it is mediated through the dramatic portrayal of the Lord's death. Some of the liturgies—Episcopal, Anglican, or Reformed—can help us here; we should carefully use them or create biblical forms and exhibit more wonder at what we are doing in the Lord's Supper.

Q: What do you think our biggest failure is in worship today?

A: I think we have too many agendas we are trying to cram into one hour or one-and-a-quarter hour of worship. We are trying to instruct, train, fellowship, evangelize, build vision, and give out all the church announcements to keep the church running for a week—all in one hour. We allow many things to formulate our objectives for worship rather than focusing on the main goal of leading people into the presence of God.

Another failure is our tendency to imitate other churches' models of worship without due regard for the unique way in which the Lord may be leading our church to worship. There is too much stress on specific *types* or *models* of worship and too little stress on entering the presence of God.

Q: If a church wants to get serious about worship, what should concerned members do?

A: Visit other churches where they are doing things differently and get ideas. Don't imitate them slavishly, but do see what is applicable to your situation. The minister should ask the leaders of the church for freedom to experiment with the worship service to make it better. Also, the minister needs to make sure *he* is worshiping as he leads the people; if he is, the people will catch it.

Q: What have you found to be the greatest benefit in your approach to worship?

A: People come to worship really wounded and needy from the battles of the world. There must be a place in the midst of the battle where there is the Sabbath presence of the Lord. If church becomes just another meeting, if there is no reality in the worship service, then we are asking people simply to come to another teaching session.

One Sunday, a very old man approached me after the service. He shook my hand and introduced himself. He looked me in the eye and said, "Young man, I have my own church, and I probably won't come back here. But I want you to know something. I have not worshiped like that for twenty-five years." He had tears in his eyes.

This interview is adapted from "What Is Worship?" in Reformed Theological Seminary's *RTS Ministry* (now the *Reformed Quarterly*), Summer 1990. Adapted by permission of Reformed Theological Seminary.

Making the Most of Worship

Preparing for worship takes some time and thoughtful planning. Here are some helps:

1. Recognize: While, biblically speaking, personal worship is an extension of corporate worship, it is also fair to say that corporate worship grows out of personal worship. Therefore, the most fundamental preparation for Sunday worship is to ready yourself as a living sacrifice to God (Rom. 12:1-2) and to have a broken and contrite heart (Ps. 51:17).

Do: Ask God for a heart of worship and brokenness each day.

2. Recognize: You cannot expect to rush into church after an exhausting Saturday night and "be worshipful." A late Saturday night may at times be necessary and fun, but if you always get less sleep than you need on Saturday night and are tired in church, can you be alert and attentive to the majesty and presence of the Lord?

Do: Get a good night's rest before Sunday worship.

3. Recognize: Conscious acknowledgment of God's deity will prepare your heart for coming into His presence.

Do: *Before going to bed on Saturday night, read individually (or pray with your family) passages of Scripture that remind you of who God is. Pray that, even as you sleep, the Lord would prepare you to worship Him (Ps. 127:2).*

4. Recognize: You must have a fertile heart on Sunday morning.

Do: *Try (though it is often difficult) to spend time alone with the Lord Sunday morning before coming to church (Ps. 5:3).*

5. Recognize: You cannot prepare adequately just before worship if you are late. If you are parking the car at the stated time for the service, then you have missed the beginning of worship.

Do: *Plan to be in your seat at least five minutes before the service starts.*

6. Recognize: God is in our presence when we gather for worship; He constitutes us as a worshiping assembly (Heb. 12:23; Gen. 28:17).

Do: *Come, conscious that God is present.*

7. Recognize: What you are really doing in worship is joining with "the assembly of the firstborn who are enrolled in heaven" (Heb. 12:23). We worship with the whole of God's elect from every time and place—including the angels (Heb. 12:22).

Do: As you come into church, imagine the host of brothers and sisters (saints from all ages, and the angels) who are waiting to worship with you.

8. Recognize: There is a healthy balance between greeting friends and being quiet as the service begins.

Do: Be quiet before worship. Pray or read a Psalm, the prayer at the top of the program, the responsive reading, or a creed.

9. Recognize: Worship takes as much effort as solving a complex problem in your checkbook or playing a good set of tennis.

Do: Concentrate on each phrase spoken, sung, or prayed. Think as you worship (Mark 12:30).

10. Recognize: Worship centers on the Word read, preached, and heard, for the Word is God's living voice speaking His will to us.

Do: Listen carefully to the Word read and preached; give the sermon full attention; pray to learn from it. And pray for your preacher!

11. Recognize: Worship is much more than hearing a sermon. The first full half of the service is not "window dressing" or a warmup for the message.

Do: Concentrate on the meaning of each part of the worship as it occurs.

12. Recognize: Worship also centers on the sacraments. In preaching, we hear the gospel; in the sacraments, we *see*, *touch*, and *taste* the gospel.

Do: Participate in the sacraments, expecting to receive what they are, means of grace.

13. Recognize: Surely we come to worship for what we "get out of it." But we also come for what God gets out of it. Do not expect to be entertained but to give glory to God.

Do: After the service, ask, "Are God and I both satisfied by my (our) worship?"

14. Recognize: Worship should change us.

Do: As you leave, resolve to do one concrete thing on the basis of your worship (Rom. 12:2).

Notes

⟿

CHAPTER 1: SEEKING ONE THING OF BEAUTY

1. Augustine, *Confessions*, 8.
2. Charles Spurgeon, *Treasury of David*, vol. 2 (New York: Funk & Wagnalls, 1887), commentary on Psalm 27:4.
3. John Piper, "The Curse of Careless Worship," sermon, November 1, 1987; available online at http://www.desiringgod.org/library/sermons/87/110187.html.
4. Augustine, *Confessions*, 1.20.
5. Jonathan Edwards, "A Divine and Supernatural Light, Immediately Imparted to the Soul by the Spirit of God, Shown to Be Both Scriptural and Rational Doctrine," 1.1.
6. C. S. Lewis, *Letters to Malcolm* (New York: Harcourt Brace, 1963), 4.
7. Jonathan Edwards, *Distinguishing Marks of a Work of the Spirit of God*, in Archie Parrish and R. C. Sproul, *The Spirit of Revival: Discovering the Wisdom of Jonathan Edwards* (Wheaton, Ill.: Crossway, 2000), 68.

CHAPTER 2: WORTHY OF PRAISE

1. John Piper, *Desiring God* (Portland, Ore.: Multnomah, 1986), 84.
2. Augustine, *Ten Homilies on the Epistle of St. John to the Parthians*, 7.8.
3. John Stott, *The Contemporary Christian* (Downers Grove, Ill.: InterVarsity Press, 1995), 39.
4. Augustine, *Confessions*, 2.2.
5. Ibid., 2.3.
6. Ibid., 3.1.
7. Ibid., 3.3.
8. Ibid., 9.1.
9. Cited in Thomas A. Hand, *Augustine on Prayer* (New York: Catholic Book Publishing, 1986), 13.
10. See John Calvin, *Institutes of the Christian Religion*, 1.5.11-12.

CHAPTER 3: SOUL-RAVISHING VIEWS

1. Jonathan Edwards, *Distinguishing Marks of a Work of the Spirit of God*, in Archie Parrish and R. C. Sproul, *The Spirit of Revival: Discovering the Wisdom of Jonathan Edwards* (Wheaton, Ill.: Crossway, 2000), 68.

2. Augustine, *Confessions*, 1.1.

CHAPTER 4: THE IMPLICATIONS OF OUR WORSHIP

1. John Piper, *The Pleasures of God* (Portland, Ore.: Multnomah, 2002), 226.

CHAPTER 5: HOW TO FIRE YOUR IMAGINATION

1. Jonathan Edwards, *The True Excellency of a Gospel Minister*, in *The Works of Jonathan Edwards*, vol. 2 (Edinburgh: Banner of Truth, 1974), 958.

CHAPTER 6: DRAWING NEAR

1. Review of *Talking to Heaven*, James Van Praagh, *The New York Times*, Feb. 22, 1998.

2. See, e.g., R. Laurence Moore, *Touchdown Jesus* (Louisville: Westminster/John Knox, 2003).

3. Jerry Adler with T. Trent Gegax, "Heaven's Gatekeepers," *Newsweek*, March 16, 1998.

General Index

Scripture Index